Knowing the East

*

bulwark

√√ 103 Lamp & the Bell

baldachin
catafalque

63√ 58 The Tomb

51

54✓

105

71

The Lockert Library of Poetry in Translation
Editorial Advisor: Richard Howard
For other titles in the Lockert Library, see page 139

Connaissance de l'Est

Knowing the East

Paul Claudel

Translated with an Introduction by James Lawler

Princeton University Press Princeton and Oxford

Published by Princeton University Press,
41 William Street, Princeton, New Jersey 08540
In the United Kingdom: Princeton University Press,
3 Market Place, Woodstock, Oxfordshire OX20 1SY

Library of Congress Cataloging-in-Publication Data
Claudel, Paul, 1868–1955.
[Connaissance de l'Est. English]
Knowing the East / Paul Claudel ; translated by James Lawler
p. cm — (The Lockert library of poetry in translation)
ISBN 0-691-11868-X (cloth : alk. paper) —
ISBN 0-691-11902-3 (pbk. : alk. paper)
I. Lawler, James. II. Title. III. Series.
PQ2605.L2C613 2004
841'.912–dc22 2003064149

British Library Cataloging-in-Publication Data is available
Publication of this book has been aided by
This book has been composed in
Adobe Garamond and Nicholas Cochin
Printed on acid-free paper. ∞
www.pup.princeton.edu
Printed in the United States of America

1   3   5   7   9   10   8   6   4   2

The Lockert Library of Poetry in Translation is supported by a
bequest from Charles Lacy Lockert (1888–1974)

Drink! I give you this vase as round as the moon.

And when you are in the midst you will see the sea rise from the cup.

And with each gulp it will enter your throat with its waters, and sails will appear afar!

And when your knees begin to sag and you breathe the last drops,

The humped mountain that tops the edge with its snows will touch the middle of your brow.

And I do not call it a beverage, but it will be for your heart like the shadows of the forest.

Take it with both hands, for it is deep and full.

Take it, I say! take it! take! take!

—Paul Claudel, "Don du vase rond"

Contents

Introduction

The East that Claudel came to know was not a passing fancy. Between 1895 and 1927 he spent eighteen years in China and Japan as a tireless observer of both countries' nature, customs, art. The majority of French writers of his time were not concerned to travel or, if they did, often settled for facile exoticism. But having been born in a Champagne village and considering himself a rustic, Claudel focused a poet's eye wherever he went.

Age twenty-six when he left for Shanghai, he had been schooled in the provinces before enrolling in a Paris lycée. He passed his baccalauréat, then undertook studies in law and political science that enabled him to enter the Ministry for Foreign Affairs and, in 1893, to assume short-term consular postings in New York and Boston. Two years later he was back in Paris and preparing to leave for China. The long voyage via Suez marked the true beginning of a life of professional exile that brought him appointments on four continents and culminated in ambassadorships to Tokyo, Washington, and Brussels. Yet it was the ten-year period in China during his twenties and thirties that allowed him to find himself. He felt that, without knowing it, he had always been waiting for his encounter with the East. "There are countries we accept," he wrote, "that we marry and straightaway adopt as we do a woman, as if they had been made for us and we for them."

He was, then, still in the obscure early stages of a diplomatic career. On the other hand, alongside his studies and subsequent administrative duties, his achievements in literature were already substantial, if little known. He had written in school throughout his "haggard adolescent years" but was galvanized by his reading of Rimbaud's *Illuminations* and *Une Saison en enfer*, which appeared in his nineteenth year. "Those books opened a breach in my materialistic prison and gave me the living, almost physical, impression of the supernatural." Nothing affected him more, nor had greater life-long influence, than Rimbaud ("I am one of those who took him at his word, who had confidence in him"), whom he could not dissociate from his conversion to Roman

Catholicism on Christmas Day of the same year. Rimbaud became his gauge of visionary genius—or rather, a seminal presence.

Nevertheless Claudel turned at the same time to a figure who was the unquestionable master of the art of poetry in the Paris of his time, Stéphane Mallarmé, whose *mardis*, or Tuesday evening meetings with young poets, he attended over a period of five years and with whom he corresponded from abroad. From Mallarmé he learned subtle lessons, the most important, he felt, being the need to ask of objects their meaning. Though none of the other young disciples reduced Mallarmé's teaching to a single formula, Claudel dared to do so and frequently reverted to identical words in his essays and commentaries. "Mallarmé," he said, "was the first to place himself in front of the world, not as before a spectacle or a theme for school homework, but as before a text, with the question: What does it want to say? [Qu'est ce que ça veut dire?]" The poet should give us neither a brute description nor a fleeting impression but, as it were, the object's hidden sense, its "intention." He believed that Mallarmé had introduced a point of view of far-reaching significance; and while he could not adopt the other's ultimate philosophical despair, he too celebrated art as visionary explication.

His creative energy found voice for the first time in a short play, *L'Endormie*. Written between 1886 and 1888, it is his youthful midsummer night's dream of light-hearted and light-headed fantasy, the sources of which lie as much in popular farce as in the Shakespeare he made his own. Rowdily he stirs his muse, and already handles a non-numeric Whitmanian *verset*, rhythmic and vigorous, which will also serve his future plays and the greater part of his poetry. Thus a boisterous individuality is patent from the start. (I think of Beddoes's words a generation earlier as he endeavored to revive English theater by way of a new instrument: "Say what you will, I am convinced the man who is to awaken the drama must be a bold, trampling fellow—no creeper into holes—no reviser even—however good." Claudel, who later translated a poem from Beddoes' *Improvisatore*, was, one can surely say, such a bold trampling fellow.)

Other, and graver, plays followed in close order: in 1888, *Une Mort prématurée*, partly destroyed, of a dark mood that adumbrates his most searing drama, *Partage de Midi* of 1905; the splendid *Tête d'Or*, published anonymously in 1890, which reveals the vast sweep of a mind and sensibility that would wish to possess the worlds visible and invisible (Claudel, in a contemporary letter, remarked of its central character: "There is in man a frightful need for happiness, and it must be fed or it will devour all things like a fire!"); *La Ville* of 1893, projecting his bitter adolescent years that led in 1890 to a second conversion by a crisis "as crucifying as a great love"; *La Jeune Fille Violaine*, sketched out in 1892 and 1893 and reworked in China, which is the first version of his miracle play, *L'Annonce faite à Marie*; and finally, his "American" drama, *L'Echange*—he felt after writing it that it had exhausted America for him—in which he projects his own New York and Boston "enslavement" in the personage of Louis Laine, who, to be free, sells his wife.

The simple listing of these plays testifies to a creative exuberance that hardly lessened over the next half-century. Nor have I mentioned the admirable rendering of the *Agamemnon* completed in the United States in 1894, nor the voluminous correspondence. The sometimes troubled course of Claudel's religious life, the pursuit of his career, his far-flung travels seem to have nourished, rather than hindered, his writing. From the time he was in New York he fixed for himself a strict daily schedule that provided time for each of his interests and occupations like a monastic rule. (Indeed, during his first period in China, he decided he would become a priest and went to Saint-Martin de Ligugé on a return visit to France in 1899 to offer himself; but he judged that he was not wanted: "I was found lacking. I have lost my sense and purpose . . ."). His departure for the East was nevertheless felt to be a deliverance, so that he could consider himself a discoverer in the wake of Rimbaud, who had likewise shaken the dust of the West from his feet so as to embrace a new world, announcing "rough-skinned reality." Claudel's resolve was no less strong: "A fissure had opened between past and present." "Separation has taken place, and the exile on which he entered follows him." Never again would he be his former self. Was he not called to articulate the East's wish-to-say?

Knowing the East is not a "book" as the Symbolists used the term. The sixty-one pieces do not form a tight artistic construction but were written one by one in the ten years that Claudel spent in Shanghai, Hankow, and, above all, his beloved Foochow, but also during a rich three-week visit to Japan in 1898. When he brought them together, in 1907, he respected the chronological order, which is that of the original publication of a good number of pieces in *La Revue blanche* and the *Mercure de France*, under titles such as "En Chine," "Paysages de Chine," and, generically, "Quatre petits poèmes" and "Quatre poèmes en prose." In letters to friends and family and in later interviews, he had recourse to similarly general terms—"images," "impressions," "drawings," "exercises"—or the collective designation "descriptive literature"; while his father, whom Claudel had asked to help place some of his early texts with Paris journals, spoke of travel notes ("notes de voyage"), no doubt adopting another of the poet's own terms. I take this hesitation to be evidence of his continuing search for means and ends in the absence of any argument or a preconceived plan.

Claudel had not previously turned to prose. Apart from agile observations in a few pages devoted to the Isle of Wight some years earlier, he had kept to drama and a small number of poems, and confessed an inherent clumsiness outside the realm of verse. Measuring himself against Mallarmé, Rimbaud, and his friend Jules Renard, as well as against those who in his view had been the supreme practitioners of French prose—Rabelais, Bossuet, Saint-Simon, Chateaubriand, Balzac, Maurice de Guérin, Michelet, but not Voltaire! not Flaubert!—he felt he had everything to learn. He told a friend in 1896, "I have never in my life written a sentence that satisfied me, never given complete expression to a statement accompanied by the order and legitimate apparatus of images and accessory relationships that make a sentence." The manuscripts of *Knowing the East* reveal a laborious genesis, whereas the author of more mature years seldom sought to revise. His aim clearly was not to elaborate one dominant style, like Gide or Proust, but to develop in each of his pieces a mode, an accent, a sustaining idea. *Knowing the East* comes fifty years after Aloÿsius Bertrand's *Gaspard de la nuit*, thirty years after Baudelaire's *Le Spleen de Paris,* both of which, in wholly different ways, had inaugurated the prose poem in France: short, dense, as heady as the combination of lyricism and abstraction or, to use the imaged polarity that Valéry elaborated, dancing and walking: the agonistic genre par excellence. No less than the complementary voices of Bertrand and Baudelaire, the "painted plates" of Rimbaud could be a model, in the same way as Mallarmé's intellectual playfulness and Renard's down-to-earth solidity: all these might be incorporated into the poet's vision, still others appropriated. The range is vast. We have only to choose a handful of texts, say the first half-dozen, to find as many styles and registers, lyrical, descriptive, and reflective. And let us not forget the peasant humor, most delectably in "The Pig," nor the bizarre, far-ranging reveries of "Dreams," nor the meditative calm of "Hours in the Garden."

Such modal diversity goes hand in hand with a large gamut of themes. With what pleasure do we savor these landscapes, this continent so far removed from our own: coconut palms, banyans, Japanese pines; the Yang-tse of "Drifting," "The River," "Halt on the Canal"; Confucian, Buddhist, and Shinto temples and tombs; hermitages, suspended houses; crushing heat, night as clear as day; festivals for the dead, a festival for the rivers; wheat harvests, rice harvests; torrential rain, apocalyptic storms; cities that seem chaotic but have a concealed pattern and sense; "flayed" Chinese gardens, the Shogun's golden ark. One may label the images picturesque but that is not the way I read them. I recall Julien Green saying of Claudel that he was a man "who had known how to live elsewhere," words I take to mean that we do not find a quest for oddness but affectionate deployment fold by fold of a reality the poet comes to know. "To enjoy is to understand," he observes in *Knowing the East*, "and to understand is to number." Every hair of the head . . .

At the center is a man in movement: "I get out of my carriage . . . ," "I enter the city . . . ," "We go up, down . . . ," "Coming out barefoot on the verandah . . . ," "Having climbed for a day. . . ." He goes in rickshaw, sedan-chair, boat, best of all on his own two feet, and poetry accompanies him. "I am the Inspector of Creation, the Verifier of things present; the solidity of this world is the matter of my beatitude." As a child, he had felt the need to escape; as a student, he had enviously watched boats passing down the Seine; he had itched to get away from his first appointment, which took him, not to some foreign port as he had hoped, but to the Quai d'Orsay. "The young people of today want to arrive. I have never wanted to do anything but leave." Again, "Who would wish to stay stupidly at home when each morning he has the entire world at his disposal?" His official functions, by their nature, seemed to command him to fit into a square hole, but it was not to be. There are anecdotes galore of his nonconformity, his glorious absent-mindedness. In *Knowing the East* he chafes at the bit, anxious to get away from the stylish evenings of the Western colonists: "a ball where for several hours I watched human bodies, some in black sheaths, others in strange flags, revolving two by two (each face expressing an incomprehensible satisfaction) to the gymnastic modulations of a piano." But afterward he is able to go back home in the night and pouring rain, and give himself to the wonder of a magnolia, "wholly decked in its great ivory lamps." He is the explorer, the "eternal pedestrian," "drunk from looking." He wants to experience everything for himself and, on one occasion, finds that he has been left behind in a dark temple, having tarried too long—incongruously, we think—to look for the twenty-seventh idol of the "Years-of-Human-Life." No explanation is given; then we remember he was at the time age 27. The detail is slight, even negligible, but I take it to typify his passionate involvement in the scene, and the scene in his spiritual quest. The same is true of "Pagoda," which intersperses description with short comments like a brisk chorus ("I walk in the December light . . . I go into the second court . . . I see the middle temple from behind . . . I do not know its name"). He sought to see things as on the first day: "I have preferred the unknown and virginal, which is the eternal." So he confronts eternity with every step: "The air is so fresh and clear I seem to walk naked." Going from sensation to meaning, and from image to symbol, he finds that the world is "adapted to our soul."

Yet this progression, still more than wilful, is sensuously impelled. Francis Ponge describes the Claudel of *Knowing the East* as "a great marine tortoise, at the other end of Asia, diving towards its Chinese salad of black mushrooms." Ponge strikes the right note: the Claudelian appetite is almost comically huge. We see him in "Drifting" lying face down in the river, moored against the current of the Yang-tse, welcoming the full flood of its waters with open arms; in "The Yellow Hour," crossing the fields up to his neck in a golden harvest; in "Libation to the Coming Day," swimming—again, naked—in a thermal spring high on the mountain, and giving himself to Aurora "like a grape seed in a glass of champagne." It is not for nothing that he makes the pig the subject of one of his most plastically achieved prose poems, which emblematizes his desire for happiness here and now as rightful possession. Hence the recurrence of terms of orality; and hence the special place in his work of the Psalmist's command: "Open your mouth and I will fill it." He quotes the words and echoes the thought constantly, without hiding the sexual charge of open-mouthed joy. It is true, on the other hand, that *Knowing the East* is underwritten by much turmoil; that at these moments it develops a somber resonance; that during the ten years of its writing its author could accuse himself of "sloth," "evil thoughts," "temptations," even "a great temptation concerning the Church"; nor can we forget the large place of funeral ceremonies and commemorative rites, graveyards, the tombs of emperors and shoguns, the poet's presentiment of his own end. Here, meditations on the myriad dead of a non-Christian world; there, flashes of cruel self-awareness ("I stand in chaos; I am lost in the belly of Death." "Let me not perish before the most golden hour.") But buoyancy reasserts itself like a renewed grace with disconcerting speed (I think of Gerard Manley Hopkins's comparable mental strife a decade earlier as he passed abruptly from the "fell of dark" to the "gold vermilion" of a "world charged with the grandeur of God"). So, in *Knowing the East,* we hear an at-times anxious, yet much more frequently exhilarated Claudel, his hope foremost: "The world's magnificence is such," he writes, "that one expects at any moment to find the silence shattered by the frightful explosion of a cry, the *ta-ra-ba* of a trumpet, the delirious exultation, the drunken elucidation of the brass." He must spell out in his poetry the sum total of his involvement.

Nor does nature alone move him, but customs, observances, temples, religion. In this way he portrays Buddhism in "The Temple of Consciousness" by the image of the path that leads to a mystical point, around which mountains and clouds range themselves and compose a scene that, as it were, takes on self-awareness. Elsewhere, in "Here and There," Buddhism is criticized for its quietude, its enjoyed nirvana, its embraced nothingness. These remarks come, however, at the end of a dazzling piece on Japanese art and thought so that we hear them not as narrow judgment but reaffirmation of the poet's own faith despite Buddhism's aesthetic and abstract seductiveness. He is not a latter-day Romantic turning to some idyllic art of wisdom, nor, assuredly, like a few of his contemporaries, a proto-fascist who uses China and Japan to condemn Western decadence. Must we not rather say that, though he is firmly attached to his own religion, country, and language, his feelings for the East are deep and strong, and—I venture the word—of the order of a sumptuous love?

But what allows us to say that his texts are poems? First, I would suggest, as for all poetry, the immediacy of the language. The themes are put to us, as it were, overabundantly; they multiply threads, interlace images and sounds, weave a close-knit texture. Each time, from the beginning, we are engaged: "It is raining softly; night has come . . . ," "It is half-past three. White mourning . . . ," "Just as there are books on beehives, the cities of birds' nests . . . ," "This is the most golden hour . . ." The opening gambit is abrupt, and we well appreciate that Claudel should have associated creative discovery with disturbance and followed Littré, quoting the German philologist Dietz, who derived "trouver" from the Latin "turbare." His challenge is to make order from disorder, to establish the scheme. To this end he has at his disposal the widest vocabulary of any of the great French poets, which reflects no doubt in part his admiration for Shakespeare's "magical casement of dream and action," found by him while still a youth. *Knowing the East* has recourse to a lexicon of huge proportions: rare Greek terms (hécatonchire), Latinisms (suspicieux), Chinese (foumao), archaisms (gautier), technical terms (libration). Such opulence, one must immediately add, is set on a base of plain, concrete words—"ready, as they call up other words, to teach what they want to say," as he notes concerning Biblical language. Thus, in "The Temple of Consciousness," we read, "The sun sets. I climb the white velvet stairs strewn with open pinecones, like roses." This diction is not of the head but of the heart. One has difficulty in fathoming Paul Souday, the influential critic of the daily *Le Temps,* who, though humorously, observed of Claudel's work, "You would always say it is translated from the Hungaro-Finnish or the Tartar-Manchurian."

Poetry is, then, achieved in a language that intermingles plain with ornate, concrete with abstract. But if critics have tended to connect the invention and development of the French prose poem with the historical turning point in painting contemporary with Manet, Claudel uses music in characteristic fashion to qualify the visual. *Knowing the East* develops its subjects by motifs and countermotifs like his greatest lyrical work, *La Cantate à trois voix* of 1913, and his greatest play, *Le Soulier de satin* of 1924. Here music shapes the prose to give us not only sonorously achieved sentences whose acoustic patterns are derived above all from Rimbaud but also some of the most structurally coherent pages in French; for this, too, is music. Valéry had Claudel in mind when he designated a "littérature de substitutions," holding that Claudel's prose can be taken apart segment by segment—"the literature of those who do not know what to say, and strong in their desire to write." Yet, where Valéry aimed at rigorous necessity, Claudel, intuitively, yet in all self-awareness, opted for a nonrational art of juxtaposition. "My thoughts do not follow each other logically," he said, "they provoke one another harmoniously."

His goal is not to argue but compose. We remember, for instance, that four of the five paragraphs of "Salutation" are introduced by "And" as a syntactic continuity that recalls the Book of Revelation ("And I saw . . . And I saw . . . And no man . . . And I wept . . .") and Hugo's "Dieu" ("Et je voyais . . . Et je sentais . . . Et l'explication, je te l'ai dit . . ."). The poet embraces past, present, and future, his port of arrival being a land like the Old Testament's Gessen and Canaan, as bold as the fields, mountains, and river before his eyes. Without narrative or descriptive support, he writes a hymn punctuated by both regret and impatience, the emotions of a man deprived of the being he loves and of the life he would embrace. He modulates his troubled self, greets a red sun reflected in the rice paddies at the beginning of his poem and a red sun at the end—now consummation, now separation. The structure couples joy and sadness on the single insistent auditory and emotional motif of the love of nature, which renews his love of God.

No less rich, "The Sedentary" follows the cycle of evening, night, dawn, midday, late afternoon. We read an intimate drama of the self as it evolves in relation to the canonical hours, each of the three paragraphs finely adjusted to the others. The poet confronts darkness—"I lie down naked at full length with my face to the night"—which becomes his nuptials with a manner of death. Nevertheless—"But . . ."—he wakes in a dawn as ravenously beautiful as a resurrection. "But . . ."—once more the poem turns—noon brings the brilliance of a sacrificial fire devouring all things—for him, a mythical death, like the leaf devoured by the silkworm, the paper by the ink. And the afternoon has a kindly, beneficent warmth—"ardent sweetness," "paternal love"—so that he goes back to his room on the topmost floor. His thoughts have been purged by light, and he is led to consider again the age-old image of life as a journey in the perspective of the book he is reading—Aquinas's *Summa*—and of the boats passing along the river at the bottom of his street. "But . . ."—one final turn—he decides that he will no longer dream of an angelic end or term, Aquinas's *finis sive terminus*, but hold to the concrete here and now. The motif runs deep: these adversatives tied to a temporal progression compose a song of praise true to feeling and melodic line.

The schemes of "Salutation" and "The Sedentary" do not, however, recur as such in *Knowing the East*, for Claudel is continually experimenting with a grand cluster of forms. Thus "The Upper Sea" proposes an affirmative, a concessive, a series of alternatives—"One day . . . ," "Certainly . . . but . . . ," "I shall then play . . . ," "Or, unlacing my shoe . . . ," "Or, cupping my hands . . ."—which open interrelated figures of the sacred, "like a man who hears his name called in a dream and tries to break his bonds." In similar fashion, the four paragraphs of "October"—"a silent, solitary concert," as Mallarmé might observe—contain the negatives and answering affirmatives of refusal and acceptance, appearance and reality, introduction and ending: "A loving response. . . ." Claudel's prose would wish to be heard as the variations on a theme.

The analogy to music is no less strong, I think, with respect to the use of metaphor. I take the first piece of the collection written during the outward voyage to Shanghai after an unplanned nine-day stopover in Colombo. In five paragraphs that, as usual, assume a stanzaic function, "The Coconut Palm" employs an over-determined language typical of *Knowing the East*. While trees in the West are solitary, the banyan reaffirms its link with the earth by means of each of its branches and thereby builds a temple. Likewise, the coconut palm shows its heart, cradles its fruit, thrives in the company of sun, water, sky—it "yields to the weight of its freedom," "sways to the earth's dreaming," and is "overcome with love." Trees, landscape, and poet participate in an encompassing tenderness.

A resonance of a similar kind is found in "November," which metaphorizes a time of emotional fervor by way of the sunset. One after the other, the images of late afternoon harvest are told, then highlighted by the splashed color and eccentric detail of two peasant farmers as they go about their chores. The poet himself follows the fiery sun in pursuit of his goal. A family is picking olives, oranges grow in the trees, voices are calling in the foliage: the description moves from great to small, small to great, after the fashion of a branch profiled against the sky. Though the sun has faded, the moon is a gentle sun he can look at, like fire revealing marine depths or some magic force abruptly conjuring up a band of foxes that welcome the poet and include him in their games. The sequence of illuminations becomes oneiric fantasy. Still he walks on, until he can at last glimpse in the far distance a new light in the valley, this time neither sun nor moon but their homely reflection in the form of a human fire. In this fashion the poem unfolds a self-echoing series of interconnected images.

We may also turn to a much longer piece that I take to be one of the volume's highest achievements. "The Golden Ark in the Forest" was written during a visit to Japan in June 1898 after Claudel had spent two days at the great Shinto and Buddhist shrine of Nikko. The title suggests a sacred wonder, and his poem opens out into ten paragraphs that vary in length from a single sentence to thirty lines and juxtapose the great and small. The guiding element is the poet's self who lends the momentum of a personal discovery in time ("When I left Yeddo. . . . At afternoon's end . . . in one drowsy moment, and for a long while afterward . . . in the sombre twilight. . . . Yesterday. . . . But this morning . . . evening's declining glory. . . .") and space ("I followed . . . I climbed . . . I crossed . . . I went into the golden interior. . . ."). Yet this is no plain diary, for details are interwoven with landscapes and reflections. At its poetic hub is the metaphor of the box—the box in the sailor's gallery, the imperial house, the box-like dwellings of the Japanese people in their volatile land—which sustains the poem through the successive images of heavily clouded sky, countryside edged by mountains, grove of clyptomeria, Gate of Sunlight, temples, the shogun's chamber, the ark. A concert of echoes is heard in the haze of reverie ("the black abyss from which our dream visions arise"), fused sight and sound ("the dazzling waterfall here and there bursts forth from the foliage, which blends with the murmur"), pervasive dream ("the huge valley . . . filled like a god's slumbers with an ocean of trees"). Art is metaphoric accord, "limitless and closed, prepared and empty." And does not this ark also signify Japan, and the East, and all of nature constantly germinative as Claudel comes to know it?

I choose one last example, much removed in matter and form from "The Coconut Palm" and "November" and "The Golden Ark in the Forest." "Night on the Verandah" treats the night sky in a way that exorcises Pascalian "eternal silence" and "infinite space." Breaks between the paragraphs are signaled not only by regular divisions but also by dashes at the indentations, which point up breadth: the constellations spread prismatically in verbal groups that make us perhaps recall Mallarmé's *Un coup de dés* published a year earlier. The poet answers anguish by continuity (the native American legends of still-born children who live on in clam shells, images of tree frogs croaking in the night, children reciting lessons in school, vowels "bubbling"), certainty (the stars perform an orderly march, our bodies are attuned to the universe), fullness (the sky is undivided, the poet enumerates the total count of the celestial expanse on each side of his house), communion (the mirror reflects the stars, seas "develop" the constellations like a photographic bath), peace (subtropical night looks—and tastes—like salt). The poem floats in weightlessness, merges metaphors of itself in a composition whose mode is as musical as the earth and sky it represents—*velut magnum carmen ineffabilis modulatoris* ("like the supreme poem of an ineffable artist"), Augustine's words that Claudel cites in the epigraph of his *Art poétique*.

Thus the collection's strange beauty needs to be savored piece by piece. But when it is read from beginning to end, other levels of meaning become clear, such as the inflexion of motifs (solitude, crowds . . .), seasons (harvests, dog days . . .), moods (exultation, despondency, fear . . .). We realize that, if Claudel sets forth no argument, there is here something akin to an organic necessity. "One must feel," he said in a 1925 conversation with Frédéric Lefèvre, "that a drama is passing behind each landscape." Passing behind rather than overtly taking place: personal issues weigh obliquely on the writing. The asymmetry of the book in this regard is significant, for the fifty-two poems from the years 1895 to 1900 are followed by a mere nine for the years 1900 to 1905. Claudel begins with the zeal of a neophyte, but ends the first part of his book on a farewell to China that he believed to be definitive. He would quit Foochow, give up his diplomatic career, become a priest, perhaps no longer write: "Here, with me, to absolve us, is the Absolute." Nevertheless, he went back to Foochow one year later when he found he was not destined for the life of a priest and, on his return voyage, fell in love with the married woman "Ysé," with whom he lived for the next four years. The poems of the second part move brokenly to a close as he undergoes a troubled and, at times, febrile period and writes his conjuration of time entitled *Art poétique*. The lover's sufferings sustain the meditation, which transcribes experience to the parabolic "unspeakable groaning" of a force, here and now, that would intermarry all things.

However the final poems of *Knowing the East* touch some more explicitly sensitive chords with "The Full Stop," "Libation to the Coming Day," "The Yellow Hour," and above all "Dissolution," in which the loved woman—that "cruel face," "that much loved face"—is dreamt once more at the moment of his own second departure from China in an atmosphere of maritime fog and vanishing detail.

In this sense, the book is autobiographical, though once again we remind ourselves that life is here always rendered as poem. The last of the sixty-one texts is more formally determined than any that precede it by virtue of its echoing halves. Held in the block of a twelve-sentence paragraph, the metaphors of ocean, mist, and tears find a cogency though muted, a consolation though bitter. Lyricism makes use of repetition and ritual phrasing, projects the sacrament of death, gives elegiac shape to the prose. The poet "enjoys" his sorrow—that is, goes to the depths of a suffering that is not so much exorcized as understood within the context of his faith and instilled from first to last in *Connaissance de l'Est* by a manner of spiritualized eros. As Rimbaud had written, in words that remained dear to Claudel, "By the spirit we go to God."

The title he chose in 1900 when he published the first series of his poems, and which he retained thereafter, seems best translated as "Knowledge of the East" (or, as the 1914 American version has it, "The East I Know"). It would designate a stable, abstract condition. Yet continuity and concreteness are still more involved. Claudel famously pointed to a link between Greek *genoumai* and *gignosko*, Latin *nasci, gignere, novi,* and *cognoscere*, French *naître* and *connaître*. In philological terms he went astray, but the pun, or so we may call it, served him well. Claudel's texts seek to be a coming to know. ("Really and truly, the angle of a triangle knows the other two angles in the same way as Isaac knew Rebecca.") To write is to understand oneself in relation to the world, and the world in relation to us—or rather, in the erotically charged immediacy of an enactment of presence. He published "Connaissance du temps" in 1904 and, three years later, coincidently with the complete edition of *Connaissance de l'Est*, "Traité de la co-naissance au monde et de soi-même," the first two sections of his *Art poétique*. Arguing for poetry as illumination, or "ah! awareness," a term he later adopted from Buddhist texts, he developed the unwritten lessons of his Oriental poems. "A matrix work," he wrote, "a book I feel to be pregnant with other books." In the Claudel canon his elliptic *Art poétique* is indeed central. It is, however, appropriate to emphasize that *Connaissance de l'Est* must rank still more eminently as a matrix work since it not only inspired the thought of *Art poétique* but also brought to accomplishment for the first time Claudel's idiosyncratic yet non-doctrinaire, physical yet spiritual "knowing."

To this book we can apply the key words of *Art poétique*: "I call knowledge very correctly the necessity for everything to be a part: first of all." We think of Claudel's vital accord with objects and people of the East: no person and no one thing suffices unto itself, for all are called to combine in a metaphoric arrangement, like tree, sky, flowers in "The Coconut Palm." "Secondly, man's freedom to play his part, to create his position in the whole." Claudel, not passive but urgently moved, participates in the drama played, the concert performed, the undiscovered ultimate melody pursued. Again: "Thirdly, that repercussion, which is knowing what one does." He was convinced that poets are born, not made; that Rimbaud was right to say that brass cannot be blamed for finding itself a trumpet; that true poetry is never written with a precise intention in view. "One must not write on purpose." *Knowing the East* goes beyond any preplanned goal by the vigor of its language, harmonies, unpredictable structures, inscape (again the Hopkins reference imposes itself). On the other hand, he called it his "most Mallarméan" work inasmuch as it implies throughout its length a unitary sense. Instead of Mallarmé's Ideal, Claudel's God. It behoves the poet retrospectively to understand the end his poetry has sought, its wager having been no less than to grasp by way of the East the bond between the cities earthly and divine.

James Lawler

Biographical Notes

1868   Birth of Paul-Louis-Charles-Marie Claudel, the third child of a middle-class family, at Villeneuve-sur-Fère in North-East France (August 6th). His elder sister Camille (1864–1943) will become a student of Rodin's and a remarkable sculptor.

1880   The year of his First Communion marks the end of his religious practice.

1881–85   After studies in the Eastern provinces, at Bar-le-Duc, Nogent-sur-Marne, and Wassy-sur-Blaise, enrolls at the Lycée Louis-le-Grand in Paris, where he acquires an excellent knowledge of Greek and Latin.

1885   Begins law studies.

1886   Reads Rimbaud, "a capital event." He later writes, "The least fragment of Rimbaud affects me in the same way as Wagner's music has always affected those of my generation." On December 25th, during Mass at Notre-Dame de Paris, returns to the Catholic faith: "In a moment my heart was touched and I believed."

1887–89   Pursues studies in law and political science. Attends Mallarmé's "Tuesdays." Begins to write plays and poetry.

1890   Appointed to the Ministry for Foreign Affairs.

1893–95   Holds junior consular posts in New York and Boston. "I have always had the desire to leave the place where I was, and to roam the world."

1895–96   Vice-consul in Shanghai. Temporarily in charge of the vice-consulate in Foochow, "that paradise of color."

1897	Plays important role in negotiating French participation in the construction of the Hankow-Peking railway.
1898	Travels in China and Japan. Goes to Foochow as vice-consul.
1899	Returns to France by way of Syria and Palestine.
1900	At the end of a year's leave during which he stays for a time at the Abbey of Solesmes and the Benedictine monastery of Liguge with a view to becoming a priest or a monk, takes up duties once more at Foochow. On the return voyage to China encounters Rosalie Vetch, his "Ysé." She figures in the background of the last poems of *Connaissance de l'Est*; she is also the model of many other figures in Claudel's works. "Why that woman? Why woman, suddenly, on that boat?" Again: "Here in your arms, Adam, is the promise—you know and she knows—that she is forever unable to fulfill."
1905	Paris. Travels in France.
1906	Marries Reine Sainte-Marie-Perrin, daughter of the architect of the Basilica of Fourvière in Lyon. Leaves for China for the third time to be consul in Tientsin, "a harsh place."
1907	Birth of the first of five children of his marriage.
1909	Returns to France on the Transsiberian. Takes up a consular appointment in Prague.
1911	Consul general in Frankfurt.
1913	Consul general in Hamburg.
1914	Expelled from Hamburg at the outbreak of the war.
1917	Chargé d'affaires in Rio de Janeiro. "Life is beautiful. . . ."
1921–27	Ambassador to Japan, where he appreciates "the sensation of a presence around us that requires ceremony and attention."
1923	Tokyo is devastated by an earthquake. Some of Claudel's manuscripts are burnt in the ensuing fires.

1927   Having passed through Hong Kong, writes a farewell to China, "a land full of bitterness and delight." The poem will be incorporated as a preface to *Connaissance de l'Est* from the 1928 edition.

1927–33 Ambassador to the United States and Canada.

1933–35 Ambassador to Belgium.

1933–55 Devotes himself to the task, begun in 1927, of interpreting and translating the Bible. "I live on my knees in the ever-growing vertigo of the Sacred Books."

1940–45 Spends the war years in his home at Brangues, in southeast France.

1955   Dies (February 23rd). State funeral at Notre-Dame de Paris. Burial at Brangues.

        His grave bears the inscription, "Here repose the remains, and the seed, of Paul Claudel," and stands by a small Japanese garden.

Note on the Text

The first edition of *Connaissance de l'Est,* comprising the poems dated 1895–1900, was published by the Mercure de France in Paris in 1900. The second, of 1907, added nine poems from the period 1900–05. The "canonical" text was not established until 1914, when a deluxe edition on rice paper was printed in Peking (today's Beijing), having been seen through the press by a fellow poet and diplomat, Victor Segalen. Several other editions followed, the most significant being those of the Gallimard *Oeuvres complètes,* volume 3 (1952), the Club français du livre (1952), which includes five previously unpublished texts, and the *Oeuvre poétique* in the Pléiade (Gallimard edition, 1957). Most useful for our purposes, the critical edition prepared by Gilbert Gadoffre appeared at the Mercure de France in 1973. It is an indispensable tool that collates the variants through the early versions.

I am much indebted to the Société des manuscrits des auteurs français for permission to consult the poet's drafts.

For further details, we may turn to remarks made by the poet as reported in Frédéric Lefèvre's *Les Sources de Paul Claudel* (1927) and in radio talks with Jean Amrouche under the title *Mémoires improvisés* (1954, and, in a much improved version, 2002). Other background material may be gleaned from the full and wise biography by Gérald Antoine, *Paul Claudel ou l'enfer du génie* (1988); from the poet's *Journal* (two volumes, Pléiade, 1968–69); and from studies by Jacques Houriez that draw on unknown or little-known materials: the critical edition of *Le Repos du septième jour* (1987), *Les Agendas de Chine* (1991), *Livre sur la Chine* (1995), and *L'Arsenal de Fou-Tchéou* (1995), all published by Les Belles Lettres, Paris. Claude-Pierre Perez has written an alert essay, *Le Défini et l'Inépuisable* (Paris: Les Belles Lettres, 1992); while the first of a two-volume study, *Genèse de la poétique de Paul Claudel* by Didier Alexandre (Paris: Champion, 2001), richly argued, is the most recent analysis.

I have mentioned in the "Introduction" an American version that appeared in 1914 at Yale University Press. The title chosen by the translators, Teresa Frances and William Rose Benét, was *The East I Know*, which emphasizes the fixed nature of the work. The translation shows many signs of haste (see my remarks, "En traduisant *Connaissance de l'Est*," *Bulletin des Etudes claudéliennes*, no. 159bis, 2000).

I thank Renée Nantet-Claudel and Henri Claudel, whose support has been a constant source of encouragement.

I gratefully acknowledge permission to include my translations of "Night on the Verandah" and "October," which first appeared in *The Yale Book of Twentieth-Century French Poetry*, ed. Mary Ann Caws, Yale University Press, 2004.

My warm thanks go to Charlotte and Daniel Levrard for help in preparing the manuscript, and to Richard Pevear for kindly advice.

Finally, I remember with affection the several Japanese students who, during the three semesters I taught in Tokyo, enabled me to hear more than one echo of Claudel.

Knowing the East

1895–1900

The Coconut Palm

Every tree of ours in the West holds itself upright like a man, though motionless; its roots thrust in the soil, it stands with outstretched arms. But here the sacred banyan does not rise singly: by pendent threads it seeks again the fertile soil and seems a temple self-engendering. Yet it is of the coconut palm alone I wish to speak.

It has no branches; at the top of its stem, it lifts a tuft of fronds.

The palm is the insignia of triumph: aerial, spreading its crest on high, it soars and expands in the sunlight where it plays, and yields to the weight of its freedom. In the warm day and long noon the tree in ecstasy parts its fronds and, at the points where they separate and diverge, there appear the great green heads of fruit like children's skulls. In this way it makes the gesture of showing its heart. For it reveals itself wholly, and the lower leaves hang down, and the middle ones spread as far as they can to each side, and those above, raised aloft, slowly make a sign as of a man who knows not what to do with his hands or signals his surrender. The trunk is not rigid but ringed, and supple, and long like a blade of grass; it sways to the earth's dreaming, whether it rises directly toward the sun or bends its tuft above swift loamy rivers, or over sea and sky.

At night, as I returned along the beach foaming with the thunderous leonine mass of the Indian Ocean driven by the southwesterly monsoon, and followed the shore strewn with fronds like the skeleton wrecks of boats and beasts, I saw on my left, through the empty forest and beneath an opaque ceiling, the image of enormous spiders climbing obliquely across the twilight sky. Venus, like a moon bathing in the purest rays, cast a broad reflection on the waters. And a coconut palm, bent over sea and planet like a being overcome with love, made the sign of bringing its heart to the heavenly fire.

I will remember that night, when I turned back on leaving. I saw heavy tresses hanging down and, across the huge peristyle of the forest, the sky where the storm set its feet on the sea and rose up like a mountain, and the pale ocean level with the earth.

I will remember you, Ceylon! Your leaves, and flowers, and soft-eyed people naked on your highways that are the color of a mango's flesh, and the long pink flowers the rickshaw man placed on my knees as, with tearful eyes and seized with pain, I rode along under your rain-soaked sky, chewing a cinnamon leaf.

[July 1895]

Pagoda

I get out of my carriage, and a frightful beggar marks the beginning of my way. With his one bloodshot eye he looks at me, and his leprous lip shows to their roots teeth as yellow as bones and as long as a rabbit's. The rest of his face has gone.

Rows of other poor wretches line both sides of the road, which is thronged at this city outlet by pedestrians, porters, and wheelbarrows laden with women and bundles. The oldest and fattest of the men is called the King of Beggars. They say that, crazed by the death of his mother, he carries her head about with him under his clothes. The last ones I notice, two very old women packaged in bands of rags, their faces black from the dust of roads on which at times they prostrate themselves, sing one of those plaints broken with long aspirations and hiccups that are these outcasts' professional sign of despair. I see the Pagoda afar off between the bamboo thickets and take a short cut across the fields.

The countryside is a vast graveyard. Everywhere, coffins. Mounds covered with withered reeds and, in the dry grass, rows of small stone posts, mitred statues or stone lions indicate the ancient sepulchres. Corporations and wealthy individuals have built whole edifices surrounded by trees and hedges. I pass between a hospice for animals and a pit crammed with the skeletons of little girls whose parents wanted to do away with them. It was closed when it became full; another will have to be dug.

The day is warm, the sky clear; I walk in the December light.

The dogs see me, bark, and run away. I go past the villages with their black roofs; I cross the fields of cotton plants and beans, cross the streams by old worn bridges; and, leaving the great empty buildings of a deserted gunpowder factory on my right, I reach my goal. You can hear the noise of bells and a drum.

Before me is the seven-storied tower. An Indian in a golden turban and a Parsee in a silk plum-colored one twisted like a stovepipe are going inside. Two other figures turn about on the topmost balcony.

I must first speak of the Pagoda itself.

It is composed of three courts and three temples flanked by accessory chapels and outbuildings. In the East, places of religious observance do not, as in Europe, barricade and segregate the mystery of a circumscribed faith and dogma. Their function is not to defend the absolute from outside appearances, but to establish a certain atmosphere; and the structures, as if suspended from the sky, gather all nature into the offering they make. Manifold, on a level with the earth, they translate space by the relationships of height and distance between the three triumphal arches or by the temples they devote to it; and Buddha, Prince of Peace, dwells inside with all the gods.

Chinese architecture, as it were, does away with walls. It amplifies and multiplies the roofs, exaggerates the horned corners that rise with an elegant surge, and turns their movements and curves upward to the sky. They seem to hang in the air; and the wider and heavier the structure of the roof, the more, by its very weight, its lightness grows from the massive shadow of the span underneath. Hence the use of black tiles forming deep grooves and strong sides that leave openings for the daylight to pass and make the summit bright and distinct. Their frieze, intricate and frail, stands out sharply in the clear air. The temple is thus a portico, a canopy, a tent whose raised corners are attached to the clouds; and earth's idols are stowed in its shade.

A fat gilded idol lives under the first portico. His right foot tucked under him, he presents the third attitude of meditation in which consciousness still exists. His eyes are closed, but beneath his golden skin one sees the red lips of a distended mouth whose long round opening, stretched at the corners, is like a figure eight. He laughs, and his laughter is that of a face asleep. What is it that pleases this obese ascete? What does he see with his closed eyes?

On each side of the hall, two on the right and two on the left, four painted and varnished colossi with short legs and huge torsos are the four demons, guardians of the four shores of heaven. Beardless like children, one brandishes snakes, another plays the viola, a third shakes a cylindrical contrivance like a closed parasol or firecracker.

I go into the second court. A great brass incense-bearer covered with inscriptions rises in the middle.

I stand before the main pavilion. On the edges of the roof are groups of small painted figures that seem to go from one side to the other, or climb as they chat. On the roof, at the angles, two pink fish with long brass barbels trembling and curving and with their tails up; in the center, two dragons fighting for the mystic jewel. I hear songs and the sound of bells, and see the bonzes through the open door moving back and forth.

The hall is high and spacious; four or five golden colossi occupy the background. The largest sits in the middle on a throne. His eyes and mouth are shut, his feet drawn beneath him, and one hand, held in the gesture of witness, points down to the earth. Thus, under the sacred tree, the perfect Buddha conceived himself: escaping the wheel of life, he participates in his own immobility. Others, perched above him, cherish their abdomens with similarly lowered eyes. These are the heavenly buddhas who sit on lotus flowers: Avalokhita, Amitabha, the Buddha of measureless light, the Buddha of the Western Paradise. At their feet the bonzes perform their rites. They have grey robes, large, light-rust-colored cloaks attached at the shoulder like togas, white cotton leggings; and some have a sort of mortar-board on their heads. Others show their scalps, where the white marks of *moxas* indicate the number of their vows. One after the other, they file past, mumbling as they go. The last is a twelve-year-old boy. I reach the third court by a side opening, and see the third temple.

Four bonzes, perched on stools, are meditating inside the door. Their shoes lie on the ground before them, and they sit—footless, detached, imponderable—on their own thoughts. They do not move; their mouths, their closed eyes no longer seem anything but creases and fringes of wrinkles in the wasted flesh of their faces, which are like the scars of a navel. Awareness of their own inertia is sufficient food for their thought. Under a niche in the center of the room I make out the shining limbs of another buddha. A chaotic public of idols is ranged along the walls in the darkness.

When I turn around, I see the middle temple from behind. High on the back wall a many-colored tympan depicts some legend among the olive trees. I go back inside. A great painted sculpture constitutes the rear. Amitofu rises to Heaven amid flames and demons. The lateral sun, passing through the trellised openings at the top of the wall, sweeps the dark box-like hall with horizontal rays.

The bonzes pursue the ceremony. Kneeling now before the colossi, they intone a chant for which their celebrant, standing before a bell in the shape of a cask, provides the lead measured by the beat of drums and the ringing of bells. He hits the jar with each verse, drawing a loud voice from its bronze paunch. Then, standing face to face in two lines, they recite some litany.

The side buildings serve as dwellings. One bonze comes in carrying a pail of water. I look at the refectory in which rice bowls are placed two by two on the empty tables.

I stand once more in front of the tower.

Just as the Pagoda, by its system of courts and buildings, expresses the breadth and dimensions of space, so the tower is its height. Poised beside the sky, it gives it scale. The seven octagonal stories are a section of the seven mystical heavens. The architect has skillfully narrowed the corners and lifted the edges. Each story casts its shadow beneath it. A bell is tied to every angle of every roof and the small globe of the clapper hangs outside. It is, as it were, a tied syllable, the imperceptible voice of each heaven; and the unheard sound hangs there like a drop of water.

I have no more to say of the Pagoda. I do not know its name.

[January 1896]

The City at Night

It is raining softly; night has come. The policeman takes the lead and turns to the left, putting an end to his talk of the time when, as a kitchen boy in the invading army, he saw his major installed in the sanctuary of the "Genie of Long Life." The path we trace is mysterious. By a series of alleys, passages, stairs, and gates, we come out in the temple courtyard where buildings with clawlike ridges and angular horn-like corners form a black frame for the night sky.

Dim firelight comes from the dark doorway. We go into the hall.

The inside cave, full of incense, glows with a red brightness. You cannot see the ceiling. A wooden grill separates the idol from his clients and the table of offerings where garlands of fruit and bowls of food are placed. The bearded face of the giant image can be faintly made out. The priests are dining, seated at a round table. Against the wall is a drum as huge as a cask, and a great gong in the form of the ace of spades. Two red tapers, like square columns, disappear in the smoke and night where vague pennants are hovering.

Forward march!

The narrow tangle of streets where we have entered among a shadowy throng is lit only by the open shops as deep as sheds that border it. These are the workrooms of carpenters, engravers; the street stalls of tailors, shoemakers, furriers. From countless kitchens, behind the displays of noodles and soup, you hear the sizzle of frying; from dark recesses the weeping of a child. Among stacked coffins, a lit pipe. A lamp, with a sideways flicker, illuminates strange jumbles. At the street corners, at the bends of solid little stone bridges, in niches behind iron bars, stunted idols can be seen between two red candles. After a long walk in the rain, night and mud, we suddenly come upon a yellow blind alley harshly lit by a great lantern. Blood-colored, plague-colored, the high walls of the ditch in which we find ourselves are daubed with an ocher so red they seem themselves to emit light. A door on our right is a round hole.

We reach a court. There is still another temple.

It is a shadowy hall from which there comes a smell of earth. It is full of idols disposed in two rows around three sides of the room, brandishing swords, lutes, roses, and branches of coral. We are told that these are "the Years of Human Life." While I am looking for the twenty-seventh, I am left behind and, before leaving, I think of peering into a niche on the other side of the door. A brown demon with four pairs of arms, his face convulsed with rage, hides there like an assassin.

Ever onward! The streets become more and more miserable. We go past high bamboo fences and finally, passing through the southern gate, turn east. The road follows the base of the high crenellated wall. On the other side are the deep trenches of a dry riverbed. We see sampans below, lit by cooking fires: a shadowy people swarms there like the infernal spirits.

And undoubtedly this pitiful shore represents the obscurely planned end of our exploration, for we turn around. City of Lanterns, we are once more amid the chaos of your ten thousand faces.

If we seek the explanation, the reason why this city through which we make our way is so completely distinct among all our crowded memories, we are at once struck by a fact: there are no horses in the streets. The city is entirely human. The Chinese hold as a manner of principle that animal or machine assistance is not to be used for a task by which a man can live. This explains the narrowness of the streets, the stairs, the curved bridges, the houses without fences, the winding alleys and passages. The city forms a coherent whole, an industrious mixture interconnected in all its parts, perforated like an ant-hill. When night comes, everyone barricades himself indoors; but during the day there are no doors, that is to say, no closed ones. The door here has no official function: it is merely a shaped opening. There is no wall that does not, by some fissure, allow a slender agile person to pass. The broad streets necessary for the rapid general traffic of a simplified mechanical existence would find no place here. There are only public corridors, constituted passageways.

An opium den and the prostitute market are the last things that occupy the frame of my memory. The smoking den is a vast nave, its two stories empty from top to bottom, superimposing their inner terraces each upon each. The house is full of blue smoke: you breathe the smell of burnt chestnuts. It is a deep, strong, macerated perfume, charged like the beat of a gong; it establishes a middle atmosphere between our air and our dreams, a funereal fumigation, which the client of these mysteries inhales. Through the fog you see the fires of small opium lamps like the souls of the smokers who will later come in numbers. Now it is too early.

On narrow stools, the prostitutes—their heads helmeted with flowers and petals, clothed in loose-fitting silk blouses and wide embroidered pants. Motionless, their hands on their knees, they wait in the street like animals at a fair, in the scramble and free-for-all of the passersby. Beside their mothers, dressed like them and as motionless, little girls sit on the same bench. Behind, a kerosene lamp lights the opening to the stairway.

I pass on, and take away with me the memory of a dense, naïve, disordered life; of a metropolis at once open and crowded, a single house containing a multiple family. I have now seen the city of former times, free of outside influences, where men lived in their hives in artless disorder. And indeed I had the sudden dazzled impression that I was emerging from all the past when, coming out of the double gate into the hubbub of wheelbarrows and sedan-chairs, in the midst of lepers and epileptics, I saw the glittering electric lights of the Concession.

[January 1896]

Gardens

It is half-past three. White mourning. The sky, as it were, is veiled in linen. The air is raw and humid.

I go into the city. I am looking for the gardens.

I walk in black gravy. Along the ditch whose crumbling edge I follow, the smell is so strong it seems explosive. Everything reeks of oil, garlic, grease, filth, opium, urine, excrement, and offal. I walk among a simple, cheerful people in thick buskins or straw sandals, the long hoods of the *foumao* or felt skullcaps, silk or cotton pants and leggings.

The wall twists and turns, goes up and down, and the coping, with its arrangement of bricks and open-work tiles, imitates the back and body of a dragon rampant. A sort of head tops it, from which there floats a curling fume of smoke.—I have arrived. I knock mysteriously at a small black door that is opened to me. Beneath overhanging roofs I cross a succession of vestibules and narrow corridors. I am in a strange place.

It is a stone garden. Like the old Italian and French artists, the Chinese have understood that a garden, by its enclosure, must be complete in itself and unitary in all its parts. Thus nature is adapted in a peculiar way to our thought; and thus by a subtle accord the master feels at home wherever he looks. Just as a landscape does not consist merely of grass and the color of the leaves but of the agreement of its lines with the slope of the ground, so the Chinese literally build their gardens with stones. They sculpt, they do not paint. Given that stones lend themselves to height and depth, contour and relief by the variety of their planes and features, they seem to them more congenial and appropriate to create a human setting than plants, which they reduce to their natural function as decoration and ornament. Nature itself has prepared the materials in accordance with the ways the hands of time, frost, rain have abraded and shaped the rock, perforating, gashing, probing it with a meticulous finger. Faces, animals, skeletons, hands, shells, headless torsoes, petrified wood like fragments of a congealed mass of people mixed with leaves and fish: Chinese art takes these strange objects, and imitates and arranges them with subtle industry.

This place represents a mountain slashed by a cliff, to which steep slopes give access. Its feet bathe in a small lake half-covered in green scum, where a zigzag bridge completes the skewed frame. Built on pink granite stilts, the teahouse mirrors in the greenish black water its triumphal double roofs, which seem to lift it from the earth like spread wings. Below, driven straight into the soil like iron candelabra, stark trees bar the sky, their giant stature dominating the garden.

I go among the stones, and by a long labyrinth whose twists and turns, ascents and evasions amplify and reduplicate the scene and simulate, around the lake and mountain, the ramblings of reverie, I reach the kiosk at the summit. The garden below me looks hollow like a valley full of temples and pavilions, and among the trees appears the poem of the roofs.

There are tall ones and low, single and multiple, some elongated like pediments and others swollen like bells. They are surrounded by friezes decorated with centipedes and fish. At the topmost intersections of their ridges the peaks display stags, storks, altars, vases, or winged pomegranates—all emblematic. Raised at the corners as you raise an outsize robe with your arms, the roofs have a chalky whiteness or sooty blackness that is yellowed and mat. The air is green, as when you look through an old windowpane.

The other slope brings us in front of the great pavilion, and the descent that leads slowly back to the lake by irregular stairs offers further surprises. At the end of an alley I see, outlined on the sky and pointing in disorder, five or six horns of a roof whose main part is hidden from me. No words can tell the drunken surge of these fairy prows, the proud elegance of these flowering stalks, which cast an oblique lily at the fretful clouds. Armed with this flower, the strong frame rises up like a bough you release.

I reach the edge of the pond, where the stems of dead lotus flowers emerge from the still waters. The silence is deep like that of a forest crossroads in winter.

This harmonious place was built for the pleasure of the members of the "Trade Syndicate for Beans and Rice," who doubtless come here on Spring evenings to drink tea and watch the glimmering lower crescent of the moon.

The other garden is still more strange.

It was almost night when, entering the square enclosure, I saw it full to the walls with a vast landscape. Imagine a mass of rocks, a chaos, a confusion of overthrown rocks heaped there by a raging sea; the vision of a place of wrath, a landscape as pale as a brain with its crisscrossed fissures laid bare. The Chinese build flayed landscapes. As inexplicable as nature, this little corner seemed no less vast and complex. From the midst of these rocks grew a dark twisted pine tree. The thinness of its trunk, the color of its bristling tufts, the violent dislocation of its axes, the disproportion of this one single tree with the fictitious country it overlooks—like a dragon bursting from the earth in a mantle of smoke, combating wind and storm—removed it from the realm of reality and made it grotesque, fantastic. Funereal leafage—here and there, yews and arborvitae in their vigorous blacks—animated the disarray. I pondered this melancholy document in amazement. And from the midst of the enclosure in the low shadows of dusk a great rock rose up like a monster and a theme of reverie and enigma.

[January 1896]

The Feast of the Dead in the Seventh Month

These cardboard ingots are the money of the dead. The figures of persons, houses, animals, are cut from thin paper, and the dead are followed by these frail images, "patterns" of life that, when burnt, accompany them wherever they go. A flute guides their souls, a gong gathers them like bees, a sudden bright flame in the dark shadows calms and satisfies them.

Along the riverbank the ready barges wait for night to come. Scarlet tinsel is fixed to the end of a pole; and whether the stream, linked to the leaf-colored sky, seems to receive its waters from on high at this bend, or it rolls its swarming mass darkly under heavy clouds, the torch blazing at the prows, the festoon of lanterns tossing at the masts vividly light the gloom as a candle you hold in a large room illuminates night's solemn emptiness. Meanwhile the signal is given: the flutes trill, the gong booms, the petards burst, the three boatsmen lean to the long scull. The boat departs and turns, leaving a line of fires in the wide sweep of its wake: small lamps, fitful glows, are strewn on the vast flood of opaque waters, which flicker for a moment, then die. An arm grasps the golden shred, the fiery sheaf as it melts and flares in the smoke, and touches the watery grave with it. The illusory brightness fascinates the cold drowned dead like fish. Other lit barges come and go; distant explosions are heard; and on the warships two bugles answer each other and together sound lights out.

The lingering stranger, seated on the shore and contemplating from his bench the huge night open before him like an atlas, will hear the religious barge return. The torches are spent, the shrill oboe quiet, but the funeral gong pursues its tumult and dance to the beat of drumsticks swollen by a continuous roll of drums. Who is drumming? The noise rises and falls, stops and starts again: now a din as if impatient hands were beating the blade hung between two worlds, now a deep solemn reverberation at regular intervals. The boat comes near, follows the bank and fleet of moored craft, then, suddenly going into the deep shadow of the opium pontoons, is at my feet. I can see nothing but the funeral orchestra that, having long been silent in the way of howling dogs, once more rends the darkness.

This is the feast of the seventh month, when the earth enters its repose.

On the road the rickshaw men have put sticks of incense and small candle-ends in the ground between their feet. I must go home. Tomorrow I shall come and sit in the same place. Everything has grown silent and, like a sightless dead man in the depths of infinite waters, I still hear the echo of the funeral sistrum and the shindy of the iron drum banging a terrible beat in the close shadows.

[February 1896]

Sea Thoughts

The boat makes its way between the islands. The sea is so calm it hardly seems to exist. It is eleven in the morning and you cannot tell whether it is raining or not.

The thoughts of the traveler go back to the previous year. He sees once more his voyage over the ocean in the night and storm; the ports, the railroad stations, his arrival on Shrove Sunday, the journey home when, with a cold eye, he looked out on the awful festivities of the crowd through the mud-spattered windows of his carriage. He would be shown once more parents, friends, familiar places, and then would have to leave again. A bitter glimpse! As if anyone could embrace his past!

That is why it is sadder to go back than to leave. The traveler returns like a guest; he is a stranger to all, and all is strange to him. Servant, hang up the coat and do not put it away! Soon he will have to leave again! At the family table, he again sits down, an unreliable passing guest. No, parents, no! This visitor you have greeted—his ears still full of the clatter of trains and the clamor of the sea, and swaying like a dreamer to the deep rhythms he still feels beneath his feet and that will again carry him off—is not the same man you took to the fatal wharf. Separation has come about, and the exile he entered follows him.

[March 1896]

Cities

Just as there are books on beehives, the cities of birds' nests, the way coral compounds are built, why do we not study human cities?

Paris, capital of the realm, even and concentric in its growth, multiplies and enlarges the image of the island which first enclosed it. London, that juxtaposition of bodily organs, stores and produces. New York is a railroad terminal. Houses have been built between the tracks, a pier, a jetty lined with wharves and warehouses. As a tongue takes in and divides its food, so New York, between its North and East rivers, has put its docks and storerooms on Long Island; while it receives and expedites the goods of Europe and its own continental West through Jersey City and the twelve railroads that align their depots on the Hudson embankment. The city's active end is wholly constituted of banks, stock exchanges, and offices, like the tip of a tongue that, just to pursue the metaphor, ceaselessly goes from one point to another. Boston is composed of two parts: on one hand, the new town, pedantic and miserly like a man who exhibits his wealth and virtue but keeps them for himself, as if the streets grew longer and more muted in the cold to listen the more spitefully to the steps of the passerby, opens up avenues on every side and grits its teeth in the wintry blast; and, on the other, the hill of the old town, like a snail that contains all the coils of shady traffic, debauchery, hypocrisy. The streets of Chinese cities are made for a people used to walking in single file, each person taking their place in the endless ranks that have no beginning; fissures have been contrived between the houses, which look like boxes with one side staved in, and the occupants sleep there pell-mell with their wares.

May there not be special features to study? The geometry of the streets, the angles of the corners, the mathematics of the junctions, the orientation of the axes? Is not everything that moves parallel to them? Everything that provides rest or distraction perpendicular?

A book.

[1896]

Theater

The palace of the Cantonese Corporation has a niche for its golden god, an inner sanctum where high seats, solemnly placed about the center, indicate rather than invite repose; and just as European clubs have a library at their disposal, so a theater has been placed with parade and pomp on the far side of the courtyard in front of the entire edifice. It is a stone terrace set back in between two buildings. The stage, a clear, tall block, is signaled only by a difference of level; it establishes a vast flat platform between the wings and the crowd below. A square canopy gives shade and consecrates it as a dais; a second portico in the foreground, framing it with four granite pillars, provides solemnity and distance. Here comedies are enacted, legends told, the vision of things that once were revealed in a roll of thunder.

The curtain, like the veil that separates us from the world of sleep, does not exist here. But as if each character, as he tore off a shred for himself, had been caught in the impenetrable cloth whose colors and illusory brightness are like the livery of night, each of them in his silken draperies shows nothing of himself but the movement that carries him forward. Beneath the plumage of his role, his golden headdress, his face hidden under greasepaint and mask, the actor is no more than a gesture and a voice. The emperor weeps for his lost kingdom, the unjustly accused princess flees to the realm of monsters and savages, armies march past, battles take place, years and distances are obliterated in a wave of the hand, debates proceed in the presence of the elders, the gods descend, the genie leaps from a jar. But never do any of the characters change their costumes, or deviate from the rhythm and encompassing recitative that measure distances and regulate action, as if all were engaged in a single chant or complex dance.

The orchestra at the back keeps up its evocative din throughout the performance as if the specters on stage, like swarms of bees you assemble by beating a cauldron, would vanish should there be silence; its function is less musical than supportive, playing the part of prompter, as it were, and answering in the name of the audience. It quickens or slows the pace, heightens the actor's speech with a sharper accent or, surging up behind him, brings to his ears the feeling and noise. There are guitars, pieces of wood that are beaten like drums or clicked like castanets: a kind of single-string violin that carries the line of the elegy on the thread of its plaintive chorus like a fountain in a solitary courtyard; and, finally, in the heroic movements, the trumpet, a sort of bugle with a wide brass opening, whose sound, charged with half-tonics, has incredible brilliance and terrible stridency. It is like the braying of an ass, a hue and cry in the desert, a flourish of trumpets addressed to the sun, a clamor belched from the diaphragm of an elephant. But the gongs and cymbals have the main role. Their raucous din stirs and predisposes the nerves, dulling thought, which lives only by the spectacle before it in a kind of sleep. Meanwhile, on one side of the stage, hung in a woven basket, two birds like turtledoves (they are, it appears, *pelitze*, from Tientsin) innocently compete with the uproar in which they bathe and pursue a song of heavenly sweetness.

The hall under the second portico, and the entire courtyard, are crammed full like a pie with live heads from which emerge the pillars and the two sandstone lions with toad-like jaws capped by children seated on top. It is a pavement of skulls and round yellow faces, so dense that the limbs and bodies are not to be seen; all participate, their massed hearts beating as one. They sway and at times, in a single movement, stretch a row of arms and are driven forward against the stone wall of the stage; at other times they withdraw and are hidden by the sides. In the upper galeries the wealthy and mandarins smoke their pipes and drink their tea in brass-saucered cups, considering both spectacle and spectators in the manner of gods. As the actors are hidden in their gowns, so the drama unfolds beneath the living fabric of the crowd as in its very bosom.

[1896]

Graves—Noises

We go up, down; we pass by the great banyan that, like Atlas, power-fully set on its contorted haunches, seems to wait with knee and shoulder for the burden of the sky. At its foot there is a small edifice where all papers inscribed with black characters are burned, as if a sacrifice of writing were offered to the stern god of the tree.

We turn, turn again, and, by a winding path, enter the region of graves. (In truth, we were in it from the time we set out, for our footsteps were accompanied by graves). The evening star, like a saint praying in the wilderness, sees the sun below it vanish beneath the deep, diaphanous waters.

The funereal region we consider in the pale light of the waning day is entirely covered with a rude yellow tuft like a tiger's pelt. From top to bottom the hills between which our path takes us, and other mountains on the further side of the valley as far as the eye can see, are burrowed with graves like a warren.

In China, death has a place no less great than life. As soon as they have passed over, the dead become important and suspect, morose, malevolent guardians, a people who are present and must be appeased. The bonds between living and dead are hard to break; the rites continue and endure. The family grave is time and again visited, incense is burnt, crackers are fired, rice and pork offered, visiting cards left in the form of a scrap of paper and validated by a pebble. In their thick coffins the dead remain within their homes for a long time, then are borne outside and piled in low sheds until the geomancer has found an appropriate site and location. The final resting place is carefully determined lest the spirits, ill at ease, wander off. The grave is dug in the mountain flank in the solid primordial earth; and while the unhappy living multitudes crowd the depths of valleys and the low-lying marshy plains, the opulent dead open their dwellings to sun and space in pleasant locations.

The burial site takes the form of an Omega applied to the hill slope; and the stone semicircle, prolonged by accolades, surrounds the dead, who doss down in its midst like sleepers under the sheets: thus, the earth, as it were, opens its arms, taking and consecrating them to itself. In front is placed the tablet indicating titles and names, for the Chinese think that a third of the soul, when it stops to read its name, remains above it. This tablet is like the reredos of a stone altar on which symmetrical offerings are laid; and, in front of it, by the ceremonial ordering of the terraces and balustrades, the grave welcomes and initiates the live family that comes on solemn days to honor the remains of the dead ancestors: a primal, testamentary hieroglyph. The hemicycle opposite echoes the invocation.

Every inch of earth above the level of the mud is occupied by these vast low tombs like the orifices of closed wells. There are small ones too, some simple, others elaborate, some new, others seemingly as old as the rocks that sustain them. The largest is on the mountain top, as in the fold of a neck: a thousand men together could kneel in its boundary.

I myself live in this domain of burial places, and, by another path, return to my house at the summit.

The city lies below, on the other side of the wide yellow Min River, which hurls its deep raging waters between the piers of the Bridge of Ten Thousand Ages. By day you see the rampart of jagged mountains surrounding the city like the fringe of graves I spoke of (flights of pigeons, and the tower in the middle of a pagoda, make you feel the hugeness of the place), bizarre roofs, two well-wooded hills rising up between the houses, and a jumble of rafts and junks whose poops are decorated with human figures like images. But now it is too dark: scarcely a single fire pricks the evening darkness below me, and the mist; and making my way by a familiar path into the funereal shadow of the pines, I gain my customary post, this great triple grave black with moss and age and oxidized like armor, which thrusts the bulk of its proud wall obliquely into space.

I come here to listen.

Chinese cities have neither factories nor vehicles: the only noise you hear of an evening, when the din of trade ceases, is the human voice. I come to listen to that; for a person who loses interest in the meaning of the words spoken around him can lend them a more subtle ear. Nearly a million people live here: I listen to the multitude talking in this pool of air. It is a clamor both torrential and sparkling, traversed by sudden loud passages like paper being torn. I even believe at times you can distinguish a note and its modulations as you tune a drum by putting your finger in the right places. Has the city different noises at various times of the day? I plan to find out. At this hour it is evening. The day's news is being widely circulated. Everyone thinks he alone is speaking, telling of quarrels, food, household events, family, trade, politics. But the words do not die away: they are carried on the numberless sum of the collective voice of which they are a part. Shorn of their meaning, they continue to exist only by the unintelligible elements of sound that bear them: utterance, intonation, accent. Now, just as there is a blending of sounds, is there also a mingling of meanings, and what is the grammar of this common language? Host of the dead, I listen for a long time from afar to this murmur, the noise of life.

But it is time to go back. The pines, among whose tall trunks I make my way, deepen the shadows of night. It is the hour when you begin to see the fireflies, those household gods of the grass. As in the depths of thought an intuition appears so quickly the mind only perceives a glimmer, a sudden sign, so an impalpable point of fire glows and, at the very instant, dies away.

[1896]

The Entrance to the Earth

Rather than assail the cliff with the iron tip of my walking stick, I prefer to view the mountains, set about me like a hundred elders in the afternoon glory, from the flat level of the plain. The Pentecostal sun lights the earth, as distinct, and ornate, and deep as a church. The air is so fresh and clear I seem to walk naked. All is peace. Everywhere you hear the harmonious note of the chain-pumps drawing water up to the fields (in groups of three, men and women laugh as they dance on the triple wheel, clinging to the beam, their faces covered in sweat), and a kindly solemn expanse opens to the walker's footsteps.

I measure with my eyes the circuit I have to follow. (I know that, from the mountaintop, the plain with its fields looks like an old stained-glass window with irregular panes set in a leaden mesh; the hills and villages stand out sharply). By the narrow dirt roads that frame the paddies, I finally come once more upon the paved way.

It crosses the paddies and orange groves, the villages guarded at one exit by their great banyan (the Father to whom all the children of the place are brought for adoption), and at the other, not far from the wells and manure pits, by the temple of the two local gods painted on the gate, both armed from head to toe and with bows at their sides, rolling their three-colored eyes at each other. And as I advance, turning my head left and right, I savor the slow passage of the hours; for, eternal pedestrian and discerning judge of the length of shadows, I miss nothing of the day's majestic ceremony. Drunk from looking, I understand all things. This bridge still to cross in the quiet peace of the afternoon pause, these hills to go up and down, this valley to traverse; and in between three pines I already see the steep rock where I must now take up my post and attend to the crowning moment of this day as it is brought to a close.

It is the time of solemn introduction, when the sun steps over the Earth's threshold. Fifteen hours ago it crossed the line of the uncircumscribed sea and, like a motionless eagle on the wing observing the landscape from afar, reached the topmost part of the sky. Now its course declines, and the Earth opens to greet it. The gorge to which it sets its mouth disappears as though devoured by fire beneath the shorter rays. The mountain, where a forest fire has broken out, sends a huge column of smoke into the sky like a crater; and over there, hit by an oblique beam of light, the line of a torrent in the forest flashes in the manner of a bolt. The Earth's Earth spreads out in the background, Asia with Europe; in the center, the high altar; the immense plain; then, at the end of it all, France like a man face down in the sea; and in the heart of France, fertile, jolly Champagne. You can now see only the top of the golden hump and, as it vanishes, it sends a dark vertical ray over the entire length and breadth of the sky. It is the time when the sea, following the sun, rises up from its bed with a deep cry and strikes the Earth with its shoulder.

Now I must go back. So high that I lift my chin to see it, the peak of Kuchang, emerging from a cloud, hangs like an island in the joyful expanses; and thinking of nothing else, I walk as if my head were separate from my body, like a man sated by the sharpness of a perfume too strong.

[May–June 1896]

Religion of the Sign

Let others find in the array of Chinese characters the head of a sheep, or hands, or a man's legs, or the sun rising behind a tree. For my part I explore a more tangled maze.

All writing begins with a stroke or line that, in its simple continuity, is the pure sign of the individual thing. The line is either horizontal, like all things that find sufficient reason for being in their sole conformity to a principle; or vertical, like trees and men, indicating an act and making a statement; or oblique, plotting motion and meaning.

The Roman letter has the vertical line for its principle, whereas the Chinese character appears to have the horizontal as its essential trait. The letter states that a thing is so with an imperious downstroke; the character is the entire thing it signifies.

Both letter and character are also signs; if one takes numerals, for example, both give us abstract images of them. But the letter is essentially analytic: every word it forms is a successive enunciation of statements that we spell out with our eyes and voice. On the same line, unit is added to unit, and the precarious vocable is composed and modified in a constant variation. But the Chinese sign, as it were, develops the numeral, and, applying it to the full series of beings, endlessly differentiates their *characters*. The word exists by the succession of letters, the character by the proportion of its lines. And may we not dream that, among the latter, the horizontal, for example, points to the species; the vertical, to the individual; the oblique, to the group of traits and energies that, in their diverse movements, give everything its meaning; the full stop suspended on the white page, to some relationship that it is fitting only to suggest. One may therefore see in the Chinese character a schematic, scriptural being that, like a living person, possesses a precise nature and moods, an activity and intimate virtue, a structure and physiognomy.

This explains the Chinese piety for writing. They respectfully burn the humblest sheet of paper marked with the mysterious trace. The sign is a being and, by its general nature, becomes sacred. The representation of an idea is here, as it were, an idol. Such is the basis of the scriptural religion peculiar to China. Yesterday I visited a Confucian temple.

It stands in a lonely district where everything smells of dereliction and decay. In the silence and solemn heat of the sun at three in the afternoon, we follow the winding street. Our entrance will not be by the great portal, the doors of which have rotted on their pivots. May the tall pillar bearing an official inscription in two languages keep the time-worn threshold! A small woman, as broadbacked as a pig, opens up side passages for us, and with echoing steps we enter the deserted courtyard.

By the proportions of the court and the peristyles that frame it; by the broad spacing of the columns and the horizontal lines of the façade; by the repetition of the two enormous roofs that raise their powerful dark scrolls together in a single movement; by the symmetrical arrangement of the two small pavilions before it that lend the pleasant bizarreness of their octagonal headdress to the severity of the whole, the building, applying only the essential laws of architecture, presents the masterly aspect of its own self-evidence, in short, a classical beauty due to exquisite observance of the rule.

The temple is composed of two parts. I suppose that the side passages with their rows of tablets on the walls, each preceded by a long narrow stone altar, provide an external series of precepts for hasty worship. But raising our feet to cross the threshold on which one is forbidden to tread, we go into the shadow of the sanctuary.

The vast high hall seems more empty, as by the effect of an occult presence. Silence, veiled in darkness, instills it. There are no ornaments, no statues. On each side of the hall we make out great inscriptions between the curtains, and altars in front of them. But behind five monumental stone blocks in the middle of the temple, there are three vases and two candlesticks; under a gold edifice, canopy, or tabernacle that frames it with its successive openings, four characters are inscribed on a vertical column.

Writing is a mystery inasmuch as it speaks. No moment marks its duration, no position the beginning of its ageless sign; no mouth proffers it. It exists; and the worshipper, coming face to face with it, meditates the readable name.

Gravely enunciated in the canopy's shadowy gold recess, the sign signifies its own silence between two pillars covered with the mystical coils of the dragon. The huge red hall imitates the color of darkness; the pillars are coated with scarlet lacquer. Alone in the middle of the temple, before the sacred word, two boles of white granite seem to bear witness and to constitute the abstract and religious nakedness of the place.

[1896]

The Banyan

The banyan pulls.

The giant of these regions does not, like its Indian brother, seize the earth again with its hands but raises itself with a turn of the shoulder and lifts its roots like coils of chains. Hardly has the trunk climbed a few feet above the soil than it stretches its limbs laboriously like an arm pulling a pile of ropes it has grasped. Slowly it spreads itself: the monster heaves, strains, works so hard in all the attitudes of toil that the bark splits and the muscles stand out from its skin. There is the thrust, the flexing and propping, the twist of loin and shoulder, the slackening of the haunches, the play of fulcrum and jack, the arms raised or lowered that seem to take the body off its elastic joints. It is a knot of pythons, a hydra relentlessly tearing itself away from the tenacious earth. You would say that the banyan is lifting a burden from the depths and holding it up with the machinery of its straining limbs.

Venerated by the humble crowd, it is a patriarch at the village gate, clad in a shadowy foliage. At its feet there is a furnace for offerings, and at its very heart where the branches begin to spread, an altar with a stone doll. There it stands, witness to all that passes, possessor of the earth it girds with its myriad roots; and wherever its shadow turns, when it is alone with the small children or when the entire village assembles under the tortuous thrust of its boughs and the pink rays of the moon traverse the openings of its canopy and light the village council with a golden backdrop, the colossus pursues its invisible toil and adds the passing moment to the accumulated centuries.

Somewhere mythology honors the heroes who gave water to the land, clearing away a huge rock and freeing the mouth of a spring. I see in the banyan a Hercules of the vegetable realm, sovereignly motionless in the monument of its labors. Is it not the chained monster that conquers the earth's greedy substance, by whom springs well up and overflow, and grass grows in the distance, and water stays at the proper level in the rice fields? It pulls.

[June 1896]

Toward the Mountain

Coming out barefoot onto the verandah, I look toward the left. On the brow of the mountain, among the torn clouds, a touch of phosphorus signals the dawn. A flurry of lamps in the house, breakfast while sleepy and numb, the packages stowed, and we are off. By the steep hill we go down to the native district.

It is the uncertain hour when cities wake. Already the open-air cooks are lighting their stoves; already a dim flickering light shows naked bodies at the back of a few shops. Despite the nailed boards placed flat on the shop fronts, people lie asleep suspended on the cornices, huddled in the corners, in every free space. Half-awake, one man scratches his side and looks at us with wide empty eyes and a delighted air. Another sleeps so heavily you would think him glued to the stones. Still another, his pants tucked up to his hips and showing a medicinal plaster fixed with a leaf to his buttocks, is urinating on the wall near his open door. An old woman, who seems to be dressed in the scum that forms on stagnant waters, combs her mangy skull with both hands. And finally I shall not forget the beggar with the head of a cannibal, his unruly mass of hair as stiff as a black bush, who lay flat in the dim morning light, one gaunt knee upright.

Nothing is stranger than a city at the hour when its people are asleep. These streets are like the alleys of a necropolis; these houses too are shelters of sleep; and everything, by its closed appearance, looks solemn and monumental. All of us, when buried in sleep, suffer the singular change you see on the faces of the dead. Like a small child with unfocused eyes who frets and feebly kneads its nurse's breast, the sleeper bites once more the deep earth with a great sigh. Everything is quiet, for it is the time the earth gives suck, and none of her children turn in vain to her generous bosom: poor and rich, young and old, just and unjust, judge and prisoner, man and beast, all drink together as kith and kin. Everything is a mystery, for this is the time men commune with their mother. The sleepers sleep and cannot wake; they cling to the teat and will not let go. That one mouthful more is theirs.

The street still smells of filth and hair.

Now the houses grow fewer. We come upon clumps of banyans, and, in the pond they shade, a giant buffalo, of which we see only the back and huge crescent-shaped horns; it stares at us agape. We pass lines of women going to the fields: when one laughs, her laughter spreads, then little by little grows less on the four faces that follow before vanishing on the fifth. When the first ray of sun crosses the virginal air, we reach the broad empty plain; and leaving the winding road behind us, we make our way toward the mountain across the fields of rice, tobacco, beans, pumpkins, cucumbers, and sugar-cane.

[June 1896]

The Upper Sea

One day as I go climbing, I reach the plateau and catch sight of the far-off Upper Sea from which dark islands emerge.

Certainly it would be possible for me to gain its shores by a perilous path; but whether I go by the edge or choose to take a boat, the surface remains impervious to my gaze.

I shall then play the flute; I shall beat the tom-tom; and the boat-woman, standing like a stork on one leg while with the other knee she holds her baby to her breast as she guides her sampan over the flat waters, will think the gods behind the drawn curtains of the clouds are disporting themselves in the courtyard of their temple.

Or, unlacing my shoe, I shall throw it over the lake. Wherever it falls, the passerby will bow down and having superstitiously picked it up, honor it with four sticks of incense.

Or, cupping my hands around my mouth, I shall call out names: first the words will die away; then the sound; then, as the meaning alone reaches someone's ear, he will turn from side to side like a man who hears his name called in a dream and tries to break his bonds.

[June 1896]

The Temple of Consciousness

I have given up more than one day to reaching it, ensconced as it is on the black rock's vertical wall, and only at this late afternoon hour do I know myself to be on the right track.

From the giddy height where I make my way, the great rice fields seem drawn like a chart, and the edge I follow is so steep that when I lift my right foot, I appear to tread, as on a carpet, on the yellow expanse of fields sown with villages.

Silence. By an old stairway overlaid with hoary moss, I go down into the bitter shade of the laurels; and as the path is suddenly blocked at one bend by a wall, I come upon a closed door.

I listen. No sound can be heard of either voice or drum. In vain do I roughly shake the wooden handle with both hands, and thump.

No bird cries as I scale the wall.

This place, after all, is inhabited; and while I sit on the handrail where the household linen is drying and sink my teeth and fingers into the thick rind of a grapefruit stolen from among the offerings, the old monk inside makes me a cup of tea.

It is not the inscription above the door, nor the dilapidated idols honored in the depths of the humble cave with a thin incense vapor, nor the acid fruit I bite that seem to constitute the religion of the place, but rather this round mat where the *bhiku* will come and squat to meditate or sleep on a low platform surrounded by a length of muslin.

Shall I not liken the vast landscape opening before me as far as the double circle of mountains and clouds to a flower whose mystic heart is this seat? Is this not the geometrical point where the harmony is composed; where it finds, as it were, existence and self-awareness; and where the occupant links the various strands each to each in the contemplation of his own mind?

The sun sets. I climb the white velvet stairs strewn with open pinecones like roses.

[October 1896]

October

In vain do I see that the trees are still green.

Whether the year is shrouded in a funereal haze or hidden under a long calm sky, we are not one day less close to its fatal solstice. The sun does not disappoint me, nor the vast opulence of the landscape; yet there is something too calm, a repose from which there is no awakening. The cricket has hardly begun its chirp than it stops for fear of being superfluous in the midst of this plenty, which, alone and of itself, takes away our right to speak; and it seems as though you can only go barefoot into the solemn fastnesses of these golden fields. No, the sky behind me no longer casts the same light over the huge harvest; and as the road leads me by the stacks, whether I go round a pool or come upon a village as I walk away from the sun, I turn toward the large pale moon that you see by day.

It was just as I came out of the dark olive trees and saw the radiant plain open before me as far as the mountain barriers that the initiatory word was given me. Oh, the last fruit of a condemned season! In the end of the day, the supreme ripeness of the irrevocable year. *It is all over.*

Winter's impatient hands will not come and roughly strip the earth. No winds tear at her, no frosts cut her, no waters drown her. But more tenderly than May, or when a thirsty vine clings to the source of life in noon's thrall, the sky smiles on the earth with ineffable love. Here now, like a heart that yields to constant prompting, is the time of consent: the grain leaves the ear, the fruit leaves the tree, the earth little by little yields to the invincible claimant of all things, death unclenches a hand too full! The words she hears now are holier than those she heard on her wedding day, deeper, richer, more bountiful: *it is all over.* The birds are sleeping; the tree falls asleep in the lengthening shade; the sun grazes the earth and covers it with an even ray. The day is done, the year at an end. A loving response is made to heaven's question: *It is all over.*

[October 1896]

November

The sun sets on a day of peace and labor. And the men, women, and children, their mops of hair full of dust and straw, their faces and legs stained with earth, are still at work. Here, they are cutting the rice; there, they are gathering the sheaves; and just as the same scene is reproduced over and over on wallpaper, so on every side you see the great rectangular wooden vats with people face to face beating fistfuls of ears of corn against the walls. And already the plough begins to turn the clay. You smell the odor of grain, the perfume of harvest. At the end of the plain busy with these farm chores, you see a wide river; and in the middle of the fields an arch of triumph, colored by the bright red sunset, completes the peaceful landscape. A man who passes nearby has a flame-colored chicken in his hands; another carries a big tin teapot in front of him at the end of his bamboo stick and, behind, a package consisting of a green bunch of relishes, or piece of meat, or bundle of the slips of silver paper that are burnt for the dead, while a fish hangs down below on a straw. His blue smock and purple trousers glow on the stubble's lacquered gold.

—Let none mock these idle hands!

The hurricane itself, and the weight of the raging sea, do not shake the heavy stone. But wood floats on water, leaves yield to the breeze. As for me, more buoyant still, my feet are not held to the soil, and the light of day, when it leaves, takes me with it. In the dark village streets, among pines and tombs, in the free expanse of the countryside, I follow the setting sun. Neither the happy plain, nor the harmony of these hills, nor the gentle green of the vegetation against the red harvest can content an eye that asks for light itself. Over there, in that square ditch girded by the mountain's rude wall, air and water burn with a mysterious fire. I see a gold so beautiful that all of nature seems to me a dead mass; and in comparison with light itself, nature's brightness is dark night. Goodly elixir, where and by what mystic path shall I be allowed to partake of your rare waters?

Tonight the sun leaves me near a great olive tree that the family it feeds are in the process of stripping. A ladder leans against the trunk; I hear voices in the foliage. In the spent, neutral glow of the hour, I see golden fruit shining in the dark vegetation. Going closer, I see each twig finely etched on the evening's heraldic green, I contemplate the small red oranges, I breathe the strong, bitter aroma. Marvelous harvest, promised to one alone! Fruit revealed to something within us that triumphs!

Before I reach the pines, night falls, and already the cold moon shows me my way. This seems to me the distinction to be made: that the sun looks at us, but that we look at the moon; its face is turned elsewhere, and like a fire illuminating the ocean depths, it alone makes the shades of darkness visible.—In the heart of this ancient tomb, in the thick grass of this ruined temple, shall I not meet a band of foxes in the forms of fair ladies or wise old men? Already they offer me verse and riddles; they make me drink their wine and forget my way. These civil hosts wish to entertain me; they climb up on top of one another—then my footsteps, undeceived, take the narrow white path that leads me back toward my home.

But already, deep in the valley, I see a human fire burning.

[1896]

Painting

Hang this piece of silk for me by the four corners, and I will not put the sky on it; nor do sea and shores, forest and mountains tempt my art. But from top to bottom and from one side to the other, as between new horizons, I will paint the earth with unsophisticated art. The limits of the communes, the divisions of the fields will be exactly drawn—those that are already ploughed and those where the battalions of sheaves still stand. I will not fail to account for every tree; and the smallest dwelling will be shown with naïve industry. If you look closely, you will make out the people: the man crossing an arched bridge with a parasol in his hand; the woman washing her tubs by a pond; the small chair borne on the shoulders of two porters; and the patient farmer ploughing a new furrow by the old. A long road edged by a double row of skiffs crosses the painting from corner to corner, and in one of the round moats, in a splash of azure that stands for water, you can see three quarters of a barely yellow moon.

[November 1896]

The Contemplative

Did I ever live anywhere but in this circular gorge hollowed in the heart of the rock? At three o'clock a crow will surely not fail to bring the bread I need, unless the constant noise of raging waters already satisfies my appetite. For, a hundred feet above, the torrent plunges as though it were violently gushing from the radiant sky itself, crossing the unexpected verge between the bamboos that obstruct it, striking with a single blow the floor of the thunderous cavern in a vertical column half-dark, half-luminous.

No human eye could find me where I am. In shadows dispersed by midday alone, my dwelling is the shore of this small lake shaken by the endless leap of the waterfall. Up there, it crosses the gap in an inexhaustible flow; but this mouthful of milk and bright water is all that directly reaches me from the bountiful sky. The stream escapes by this bend and at times, together with the birdcalls in the forest, I hear the abundant, irretrievable noise of the waters behind me as they fall to earth amid the voice of this nearby gushing.

[1896]

December

Your hand, sweeping the countryside and this leafy valley, reaches the purple and tan regions that your eyes find beneath you and, with them, rests on this rich brocade. All is quiet, muffled; no harsh green, nothing young or new mars the arrangement and harmony of these ample, subdued tones. A dark cloud covers the entire sky and fills the mountain's irregular clefts with haze: you would think it dovetailed to the horizon. Caress with the palm of your hand these large adornments stitched to the hyacinth plains by the tufts of black pines; check with your fingers the details embedded in the weft and mist of this winter day—a row of trees, a village. Time has most certainly come to an end. Like an empty theater pervaded by melancholy, the closed landscape seems to attend to a voice so high-pitched I cannot hear it.

These December afternoons are sweet.

Nothing yet speaks of a troublesome future. And the past is not so much alive that it allows nothing else to survive. Nothing remains but scattered straw and dry stubble of so much grass and so great a harvest; cold water deadens the ploughed earth. All is at an end. This is the pause, the suspense between one year and the next. With silent joy thought, delivered from toil, turns to meditation and, envisaging new projects, savors its sabbath, like the earth.

[1896]

Storm

In the morning, leaving behind a honey-and-rose-colored shore, our boat enters the high seas and patches of soft low mists. When I wake from a dark dream and look for the day, I see the sun setting behind us; but delimiting the dark, dead expanse of sea, a long mountain like a snowy slope bars the North from edge to edge; you would think it was the Alps, even Alpine winter and strictness.

Alone in the midst of the solitude, like a combatant who ventures forth into a huge arena, our boat cleaves the melancholy waters as it heads toward the white obstacle. And suddenly the clouds hide the sky from view, like the hood of a carriage: in the fissure of day on the horizon behind us, I still want to see the sun, the islands lit as by a lamp, and three junks standing on the furthest ridge of the sea.

We rush now over the arena ravaged by clouds. The level plain swings from side to side and, in accord with the marine movement in which our boat has its part, the prow solemnly rises and falls as if in salute, or like a cock that takes the measure of its adversary.

Night has fallen: from the north a harsh, horrid wind is blowing. On one side the red moon moves in the disorderly clouds, slicing through them with its lenticular edge; on the other, the beacon lamp, with its convex glass, hoisted to our foresail. But everything is still calm; the sheaf of water still gushes evenly before us and, traversed by a dark fire, like a substance composed of tears, rolls streams of water over our bowsprit.

[December 1896]

The Pig

I shall paint here a portrait of the Pig.

He is a solid beast, all of one piece; without joint or neck, he forges ahead like a ploughshare. Jolting on his four squat hams, he is a trunk at a gait, ever on the watch; and to each and every thing he smells, he applies his pump-like body and gulps it down. When he finds the hole he needs, he wallows in it hugely. This is not the quivering of a duck entering the water, nor the sociable jollity of a dog; it is deep, lone, conscious, integral enjoyment. He sniffs, sips, tastes, and you cannot tell whether he is drinking or eating. Perfectly round, he advances with a wriggle and buries himself in the unctuous bosom of the fresh mud. He grunts, luxuriates to the deep recesses of his tripery, winks an eye. An accomplished connoisseur, though his ever-active olfactory apparatus allows nothing to escape, his tastes do not run to fleeting scents of flowers or frivolous fruit. In all things he seeks nourishment: he likes it rich, strong, ripe, and his instinct binds him to two basic things: earth and ordure.

Glutton! Libertine! If I present you with this model, admit that something is wanting for your own satisfaction. The body does not suffice unto itself; and it is no vain doctrine that teaches us to apply to truth not the eye alone, but unreservedly all that is oneself.

Happiness is our duty and birthright. A certain total possession is granted.

Yet a sow, like the one that gave Aeneas the oracles, always seems to me an augury, a political emblem. Her flank is darker than hills seen through rain; and when she lies down suckling a battalion of young boars that march between her legs, she seems to me the very image of hills milked by clusters of villages that hug their streams, and no less massive and shapeless.

I do not forget that the pig's blood serves to fix gold.

[1896]

Drifting

Let other rivers bear oak branches toward the sea and the red infusion of rusty soil; or roses with the bark of plane trees, or scattered straw, or blocks of ice. Let the Seine on dark December mornings, when half-past nine chimes from the city belfry, unmoor barges of rubbish and lighters laden with casks under the still arms of the derricks. Let the river Haha, at the smoking crest of its rapids, abruptly raise the bole of a one-hundred-foot fir like a rude pike; and let the equatorial rivers carry mixed worlds of trees and grass in their turbid flow. Flat on my belly and tied fast against the current, the breadth of this river is not enough for my arms, nor its huge swell sufficient for my engulfment.

The promises of the West are not lies! Know this: not in vain does this gold call on our darkness, nor is it bare of delight. I have found that it is not enough to see, that it is not expedient to stand upright; the analysis of my enjoyment concerns that which I possess beneath me. For, coming down the steep bank on astonished feet, I have found the drifting of waters! The riches of the West are not alien to me: they flow wholly toward me, pouring down the earth's slope.

Neither the silk that is crumpled by hand or foot, nor the deep wool of a sacred carpet, can be likened to the resistance of this fluid thickness in which my body alone sustains me; nor can the name of milk or the color of a rose be compared to this marvel I receive upon me. Truly do I drink, truly am I immersed in wine! Let the ports open to cargoes of wood and grain that come down from the highlands; let the fishermen tend their nets to catch flotsam and fish; let those who fossick for gold strain the waters and sift the sands: the river brings me wealth no less. Do not say that I see, for eyes are not enough for that which needs a subtler sense. To enjoy is to understand, and to understand is to number.

At the hour when sacred night calls on the shadow it dissolves to make a total response, the surface of these waters opens an unflowered garden to my motionless sailing. Here now, between the thick purple folds, the waters are painted as with mirrored tapers, here is amber, here the gentlest green, here now is the color of gold. But let us be silent: what I know is mine and, whereas these waters will grow black, I shall possess the night whole and entire together with the full count of stars visible and invisible.

[March 1897]

Doors

Every square door opens less than its enfolding leaf closes.

Several are they who have made their veiled way to this lone sanctuary and its courtyard filled with a great silence. But if, having climbed the stairs and refrained from striking the drum placed there for the use of visitors; then, having heard their name called like a voice saddened by the distance (for the wife or son shout as loudly as they can in the dead person's ear), they overcome a fatal lethargy to the point of retreating one or two steps from the leaves of the door held ajar by the desirable fissure, their souls recover their bodies. No heard melody of a name will, however, bring back him or her who takes an irreparable step over the silent threshold. Surely this is the place where I live as I taste the hushed garden's oblivion and mystery, poised on the flat paving stone of the dark pool with its extravagant frame about me.

An old memory has not more bends and strange alleys than the path that brought me here by a series of courts, grottoes, and corridors. The art of this closed place is to hide its limits by leading me astray. Walls that rise and fall like waves divide it into different sections; and the tree-tops and pavilion roofs seem to invite their guest to pierce their secrets, alternating surprises and disappointments as he advances, leading him ever further. Let a wise dwarf with a skull like the belly of a gourd, or a brace of storks, perch on the ornamental summit of a roof, the high calyx shelters no hall so empty that it does not contain a smouldering half-burnt stick of incense or a withering, forgotten flower. The Princess or the Old Man have just left their seat, and the green air still holds the rustle of a lustrous silk.

Fabulous, indeed, is my home! I see banks of clouds in these walls where the pierced copings seem to be dissolving; and these fanciful windows are like masses of leaves perceived dimly by fits and starts. The wind, leaving curved streaks on each side, has torn irregular gaps in the fog. Let me not gather the afternoon flower in any garden but this, which I enter by a door in the form of a vase, or a leaf, or an animal snout that one sees through the vapors, or the sunset when its disk touches the sea-line and the moon rises.

[April 1897]

The River

From the vast yellow river my eyes turn back to our leadsman clinging to the side of the boat. He swings the line in his fist with a regular motion and sends the lead flying over the muddy waters.

As the segments of a parallelogram come together and meet, so water expresses the force of a landscape reduced to its geometrical lines. Each drop is the fugitive sum, the ever-growing expression of the circumferential slope; and having found the lowest point of a given area, a current forms that, with ever-greater impetus, flees toward the ever-deeper center of an ever-larger circle. This river before me is huge in force and mass. It is the point of exodus of a world, Asia in movement, that finds an outlet. As mighty as the sea, it has end and purpose. Without branches or tributaries, its flood is undivided. We shall in vain spend whole days heading upstream without reaching the fork; and forever before us, opening the earth's heartland with an irresistible volume, the river evenly cleaves the western horizon.

All water draws us; and certainly this river, more than the virginal blue sea, calls to that which in us lies between flesh and soul, our own human stream charged with courage and spirit, our blood that burns darkly. Here is one of the great working arteries of the world, one of life's routes of distribution. Beneath me I feel the movement of the plasma toiling and destroying, transporting and fashioning. And while we go up this enormous mass that bears down on us from the grey sky and is engulfed by our progress, we greet the entire earth, the Earth's Earth, Asia, mother of all mankind, central, solid, primordial. Oh fulsome breast! I do indeed see it, and the grass on all sides cannot hide it. I have penetrated the mystery. As water attests an undeniable wound by a purple stain, so the earth has impregnated this river with its substance. There is no matter left but gold.

The sky lowers, the clouds rush northward. To my right and left I see a dark Mesopotamia. No villages or tilled fields; here and there, between the stripped trees, just four or five frail huts, a few bits of fishing-tackle on the bank, a broken-down bark making its way—poverty's vessel hoisting a rag for a sail. Plague has blighted the land, and the river, as it rolls floods of life and food, waters a region no less deserted than the one seen by the waters that flowed from Paradise when man first pierced a bullock's horn and blew a rude and bitter note in the unechoing countryside.

[March 1897]

Rain

By the two windows before me, and the two on my left and the two on my right, I see, I hear with both ears the rain coming down in torrents. I think it is a quarter past twelve. Around me, all is water and light. I dip my pen in the ink and, enjoying the security of my interior aquatic prison like an insect in an air bubble, I write this poem.

It is no drizzle, no languid hesitant rain that is falling. The cloud takes hold of the earth, and tightly and roughly falls on it in a deep, heavy assault. How fresh it is, frogs—enough to make you forget your pond in the damp grass! There is no need to fear that this rain will come to an end; it is abundant, satisfying. He would be a thirsty man, my brothers, who was not quenched by this marvelous bumper! The earth has vanished, the house is awash, the submerged trees are streaming with water; the river itself, which is the limit of my horizon like a sea, appears to be drowned. I do not feel the passage of time; and when I strain my ear, it is not to catch the sign of a change but to meditate on the neutral and numberless intonation of the psalm.

Yet the rain stops toward the close of day, and while the massed clouds make ready for a more somber assault, a black spider, like Iris who sped straight from heaven into the heart of battle, comes to a halt with its head down, hanging by its rear quarters in the middle of the window I have opened onto the foliage and the walnut-stained North. It is no longer day; it is time to light my lamp. I make to the storms the libation of this drop of ink.

[1897]

Night on the Verandah

Some native Americans believe that the souls of still-born children live in the shells of clams. Tonight I hear the unbroken chorus of tree frogs like the elocution of children, the plaintive recitation of little girls, a bubbling of vowels.

—I have long studied the ways of the stars. Some go alone, others in groups. I have recognized the Gates and the Crossroads. Where the clearest space meets the topmost point, Jupiter, pure and green, advances like a golden calf. The positions of the stars are not left to chance; the interplay of their distances tells me the proportions of the abyss; their movements are part of our balance in a vital, nonmechanical way. I touch them with my feet.

—Reaching the last of these ten windows, the secret is to catch sight of another piece of the starry chart at the opposite window, across the dark empty room.

—Nothing will disturb your dreams, no heavenly glance into your room will trouble your rest if you take care, before you go to bed, to put this large mirror in front of the night. The earth only presents the stars with such a wide expanse of sea so as to offer more space for their influence, and a deep *bath* like a photographic developer.

—The night is so calm it seems to me salty.

[1897]

The Moon's Splendor

By this key that sets me free and opens the woolen door to my blindness; by this irresistible departure; by this mysterious gentleness that moves me; by this germinal meeting of my heart with the silent explosion of inexplicable answers, I understand that I am asleep, and wake.

I had left a dark opaque night at the four windows and now, coming out on the verandah, I see the whole length and breadth of space flooded with your light, sun of our dreams! Far from troubling my sleep, this fire that rises from the depths of shadow is sleep's consummation, and it overwhelms me still more. Yet I have not come in vain from my couch, like a priest for the sacred mysteries, to contemplate this occult mirror. The sun's brilliance is a force of life and creation, and our vision partakes of its energy. But the moon's splendor is like the reflection of thought. Without tone and heat, it alone is offered to me, and the whole of creation is painted black in its shining expanse. What solemn rites! Earlier than the morning, I contemplate the world's image. And already the great tree has flowered. Alone and erect, like a huge white lilac and a nocturnal bride, it trembles, dripping with light.

O after-midnight sun! Neither the Pole Star at the zenith of the vertiginous sky, nor the Bull's red fire, nor the planet at the heart of that deep tree, like a bright topaz you see when a leaf stirs—none of these is my predestined princess; but, above me, the furthest, most solitary star lost in so much light that my eye, now in rhythmic accord with my heart, just recognizes before seeing it disappear.

[1897]

Dreams

At night, when you go to a concert, make sure you order a lantern for your return. Shod in white, take care not to lose track of either of your shoes for fear that, having once entrusted your soles to an invisible path through the air and mist, the unfamiliar way leads you hopelessly off course, and dawn finds you entangled at the top of some law-court flagstaff or high on a temple wall, like a bat on the head of a chimera.

—Seeing this patch of white wall lit by the moon's blazing fire, the priest, at his rudder, did not hesitate to drive his little boat at it; and until morning the bare, bright sea nowhere showed the secret trace of his oar.

—The fisherman, having digested this long day of silence and melancholy, and the sky, the countryside, three trees, and the water, has not built expectation to such a vain degree that nothing is taken by his bait. In the depths of his belly he feels at the clutch of his hook the gentle tug of the taut line, which cleaves the still surface and carries him away toward the black ceiling. A leaf, falling backward, does not disturb the glassy pool.

—Who knows *where* you might not some day find the trace of your hand and the seal of your thumb if each night, before going to sleep, you took care to smear your fingers with some thick black ink?

—Moored to the outer opening of my fireplace, the canoe, almost vertical, is waiting for me. Having finished my work, I am invited out to tea on one of the islands that cross the sky in an east-south-westerly direction. With its clustered buildings and the warm tones of its marble walls, the place resembles a city of Africa or Italy. The sewage system is perfect and, on the terrace where we sit, we enjoy healthy air and an extended view. Unfinished buildings, ruined wharves, crumbling bridges that were never finished, surround this Cyclades on all sides.

—Since this jetty of yellow mud where we live became set in the mother-of-pearl watery plain, I go each evening to watch the progress of the flood from the ramparts; and the illusion and marvel of it all rise to meet me. In vain do the barges, from the other side of the lagoon, bring in earth to strengthen our crumbling levee. What confidence could I have had in these green path-crossed fields to which the farmer willingly entrusted his labor and seeds, if one day, having climbed up to the wall, I had seen them replaced by these dawn-colored waters? A lone village, a tree drowned up to its branches, emerge here and there; and at the spot where a yellow gang was digging, I see boats like eyelashes, and I read other threats in this all-too-beautiful evening! No stronger than an old precept against pleasure is this ruined wall where poor soldiers that guard the gates proclaim the night with trumpets four cubits long: it will not protect our dark factories or the warehouses full of hides and tallow from the evening and the irresistible spread of these azure and rose-tinged waters. Like an incoming wave that lifts me off my feet and carries me away, bearing me by my armpits . . .

—And once more I see myself in the wind, at the highest fork of the tree, a child swaying among the apples. From up here, like a god on his seat, as spectator of the world's theater, I make a deep study of the earth's relief and configuration, the arrangement of its slopes and planes; with my eyes fixed like a crow, I stare at the countryside spread beneath my perch, and follow from afar the road that appears twice on successive crests and is finally lost in the forest. But nothing is lost on me—the direction of the smoke, the quality of the shade and light, the progress of the farm work, that coach making its way along the road, the hunters' rifle shots. I need no newspaper in which I can read only the past; I have merely to climb to this branch and, looking over the wall, I see before me all of the present. The moon rises; bathed in this house of fruit, I turn my face toward it. I remain still, and from time to time an apple falls from the tree like a ripe heavy thought.

[1897]

Heat

The day is harsher than hell itself.

Outside, the sun is irresistible. Blinding splendor devours all shade, so relentless it seems solid. About me I see less stillness than stupor: arrested violence. For the earth during these last four moons has brought its generation to fullness; it is time for the Spouse to kill her and, unveiling the fire that burns within him, to condemn her with an inexorable kiss.

As for me, what shall I say? Ah! if these flames terrify me with respect to my own weakness, if my eye turns away, if my flesh sweats, if I bend on the triple articulation of my legs, I will accuse my inert body, but a manly spirit will emerge in a heroic surge! I feel it! My soul hesitates, but nothing less than the absolute can satisfy my terrible, delicious jealousy. Let others flee beneath the earth, let them carefully wall up the openings of their homes; but a sublime heart, racked by love's torment, embraces fire and torture. Sun, redouble your flames! It is not enough to burn. Consume! I would suffer not to suffer enough. Let nothing impure escape the furnace; let no blind spot escape the punishment of light!

[July 1897]

Considering the City

At a time when, driven by a high presentiment, a man without wife or child reaches the crest of the hill level with the setting sun, the solemn arrangement of the image of a city above the earth and its peoples figures the huge moment of suspense.

It is a city of temples.

In a modern metropolis you see the streets and districts pressing and congregating around stock exchanges, and market places, and schools, and municipal buildings, whose high pinnacles and coordinated masses stand out above the uniform roofs. But the image here placed of the eternal city, this monument built by evening in the form of a three-layered mountain, displays no worldly detail and, in the endless disposition of its buildings and order of its plan, presents nothing unrelated to an end so sublime that any later development is not already encompassed by its foundations.

And just as the citizen of the Kingdom whose path brings him to the capital city strives to know the plan of the enormous construction, so the contemplative, impatient to discard his soiled shoes as he thinks of Jerusalem, tries to discover the laws and conditions of the place. The naves of its churches and the system and correspondences of its cupolas and pylons do not escape the requirements of a cult; nor are the movement and details of the stairs and terraces irrelevant to the unfolding of the ceremony. The moats of the towers, the superimposed walls, the basilicas, circuses, and reservoirs, and the tree tops in the square gardens, are all made of the same snow; and the violet shade that darkens them is perhaps only the hue of mourning added by irreparable distance.

So one evening, for an instant, did a solitary city appear before me.

[1897]

Going down the River

Ah! Let these people continue to sleep! Let this boat not soon reach port! Let me be spared the misfortune of hearing or uttering a word!

Coming from night's sleep, I have woken in flames.

So much beauty makes me laugh! What richness, what splendor! What force of inextinguishable color! It is dawn. O God, how fresh for me is this blue! How tender this green, how fresh! And looking at the sky behind me, what peace, to see it still so dark that the stars are twinkling. But you well know, my friend, which way to turn and what treasure is yours if, raising your eyes, you do not blush to see this heavenly brightness! Oh! may it be this very color that I am given to contemplate! It is not red, nor the color of the sun; it is the fusion of blood in gold! it is life consummated in victory, it is the renewal of youth in eternity! The thought that it is the sunrise does not lessen my exultation. But what embarrasses me like a lover and makes my whole body tremble is the intention of this glory, it is my admission to it, it is the approach of this joy to meet me!

Drink, oh my heart, these inexhaustible delights!

What do you fear? Do you not see which way the current takes us, quickening the movement of our boat? Why doubt that we shall arrive and that a huge day will match so bright a promise? I foresee that the sun will rise and that I must prepare to sustain its power. Oh light! drown all passing things in the bosom of your abyss! Let noon come, and I shall be allowed to contemplate your reign, Summer, and to consummate the day in my perfected joy, sitting amid the peace of all the earth in the harvest solitude.

[July 1897]

The Bell

When the air rejoices in perfect stillness, at the hour when the sun consummates noon's mystery, the great bell reverberates with the earth, its deep concave expanse taken to the point of melody beneath the blows of the cedar ram. Then, retreating and advancing, crossing plain and mountain, a great wall, whose Cyclopean portals you see on the far horizon marking the symmetrical measures, circumscribes the thunderous volume of enclosed sound and draws the limits of its resonance. A city is built in one horn of the enclosure, the remaining space being given over to fields, woods, tombs; and here and there, in the shade of the sycamores, a bronze vibration deep within a pagoda echoes the now silent monster.

Near the observatory where K'ang-hsi came to study the star of old age, I saw the pavilion in which the bell is honored with offerings and inscriptions, and kept under the guard of an old bonze. An average man's outstretched arms are the span of its mouth. I knock the surface with a finger and it sings through its six-inch thickness at this slightest shock. For a long while I lend my ear. And I remember the story of the molder.

That a string of silk or catgut should resound beneath fingernail or bow; that wood, having once been taught by the winds, should lend itself to music—this did not stir the artisan's curiosity. But it seemed to him that the way to make man ring and wholly awaken the human urn was to attack the very element, to extract the musical scale from the primitive soil. And his art was the casting of bells.

The first bell he cast was taken off to heaven in a storm. The second, having been loaded on a boat, fell into the midst of deep loamy Kiang. And the man resolved to cast a third before he died.

And this time he wanted to gather together the soul and all the noise of fertile, nourishing earth into the recess of a single deep vessel, to capture the fullness of every sound in a roll of thunder. Such was his plan, and the day he began a daughter was born to him.

Fifteen years he toiled at his task. But in vain, having planned his bell, did he establish its size, curve, and caliber with subtle art; in vain did he extract from the most secret metals all that listens and trembles, and make flakes so sensitive they sounded at the mere approach of a hand; in vain did he strive to forge the properties and harmonies of a single sonorous instrument. From the sand mold in vain would emerge a clean and faultless part, for the bronze never made the expected response to his questioning; and if the beat of the double vibration was balanced at exact intervals, he despaired ever to feel life in it, or that indefinable mellowness and moistness that saliva confers on words formed by the human mouth.

Meanwhile his daughter grew alongside her father's despair. And already she saw the old man, gnawed by his mania, who no longer sought new alloys but instead threw ears of corn, sap of aloe, and blood of his own veins into the crucible. Then a great pity was born in the heart of the girl for whom women today come to the bell to venerate her image of painted wood. She said a prayer to the subterranean god, dressed herself in her wedding clothes, and, having tied a twig of straw about her neck like a consecrated victim, plunged into the sacred metal.

In this way the bell was given a soul, and the vibration of elemental forces achieved a female, virginal resonance and an unspeakable liquid tone.

And the old man kissed the still warm bronze, then struck it mightily with his mallet, and so great was his rapture to hear the sacred chime that his heart languished within him and, sinking to his knees, he could not keep from dying.

Since then, and from the day a city was born of the bell's opulence, the cracked metal has given out only a faint sound. But the sage of vigilant heart may still hear the first bell at dawn in the heavenly expanse, when a cold light wind blows from skies the color of apricots and hopflowers, and the second at dark sunset, in the deep reaches of huge, loamy Kiang.

[September 1897]

The Tomb

On the pediment of the funeral gates I read the order to step down. On my right, some sculpted fragments in the reeds; while an inscription on a giant black granite boulder gives the inane details of the laws governing the burial place. A warning, overgrown by moss, forbids vases to be broken, shouts to be given, lustral tanks to be despoiled.

It is certainly past two o'clock for I see the dull round sun ahead, a third of the way across the pale sky. I can view the arrangement of the necropolis as far as the vertical hill; and, readying my heart, I start to walk by the funeral path through this place, itself dead, and dedicated to death.

First, I come upon two square mountains of bricks, one after the other. By four arches the central cavity opens onto the four cardinal points. The first of these halls is empty; in the second, a great marble tortoise, so high I can scarcely reach its moustached head, supports the panegyric stele. "Here is the porch and vestibule of the earth: it is here," I say, "that death halted on a dual threshold, and that the master of the world, between the four horizons and the sky, received a supreme homage."

Yet hardly have I left by the northern door (I do not cross that stream in vain) than I see the land of dead spirits opening before me.

For in front of me there are animal monsters forming a path in alternate couples. Face to face, over and again in successive order, kneeling and upright, the enormous, misshapen stone blocks of paired rams, horses, unicorns, camels, and elephants stand out against the drear grass as far away as the bend, where the remainder of the procession vanishes. Further along, the civil and military mandarins are buried.

Animals and men delegated these stones for the Shepherd's funeral. And as we have crossed the threshold of life, a closer resemblance would not be fitting for such images.

Here, we are told, this broad mound hides the treasures and bones of a more ancient dynasty, and, as the way is no longer barred, our path turns east. I walk now among soldiers and ministers. Some are intact and upright; others lie on their faces; one headless warrior is still clasping his saber. And on a triple bridge the path crosses the second canal.

Now, by a series of stairways where the median strip still carries the imperial snake, I cross the devastated frames of terraces and courtyards. Here is the esplanade of memory, the flat vestige where the human foot enriched the immortal soil when it departed, the sacrificial landing, the enclosure by means of which the abolished object still solemnly testifies that it did indeed exist. In the center the throne bears, and the baldachin still shields, the dynastic inscription. Around it, the temples and imperial guesthouses are no longer anything but heaps of debris in the brambles.

And here before me is the grave.

Between the massive abutments of the square bastions edging it, and behind the deep definitive trench of the third watercourse, a wall leaves no doubt that this is the end of the way. A wall, and nothing but a wall, a hundred feet high and two hundred feet wide. Damaged by the wear and tear of centuries, the immovable barrier presents a blind brick face. A single round hole opens in the middle of the base, like the mouth of an oven, or the air hole of a jail. The wall is the back casing of a kind of trapezoidal pedestal separate from the hill above it; at the bottom an ornamental moulding goes back under an overhanging cornice, giving clearance in the manner of a bracket. No corpse is regarded with so much suspicion that it requires a huge mass of this sort to be placed over it. It is the throne of Death itself, the regal elevation of the sepulcher.

A narrow corridor going up the inclined plane crosses the mound from side to side. At the end there is nothing but the hill itself, in whose steep flank the old Ming lies deeply hidden.

And I understand that this is the burial place of the Atheist. Time has scattered the vain temples and laid the idols in the dust. All that remains is the arrangement, together with the concept. The stately catafalques of the threshold did not hold the dead man, the deceased retinue of his days of glory did not delay him; he passed over the three rivers, traversed the multiform parvis and the incense. Nor did this monument made for him suffice to preserve him; he passed through it and entered the primitive earth. It was simple burial, the meeting of raw earth with compact inert clay; man and king are forever one in a dreamless death without resurrection.

But the evening shadows lengthen over this wild place. O ruins! The grave has survived you, and the perfect sign in the brutal fixture of this solid block has survived death itself.

As I return among the stone colossi, I see in the withered grass the carcass of a flayed horse being torn apart by a dog. The beast looks at me as it licks the blood on its chops: then, again bringing its paws to bear on the red chine, it tears off a long strip of flesh. A heap of entrails is spread alongside.

[September 1897]

The Sadness of Water

There is a source of invention in joy, I agree, of vision in laughter. But, so that you may grasp the mixture of blessedness and bitterness in the act of creation, I will explain to you, my friend, at a time when the dark season begins, the sadness of water.

From the sky and the eyelid wells up an identical tear.

Do not think of imputing your melancholy to the clouds or to this veil of the somber shower. Shut your eyes, listen! The rain is falling.

And it is not the monotony of this unvarying noise that suffices to explain it.

It is the weariness of a grief whose cause is in itself, it is the travail of love, the hardship of toil. The skies weep upon the earth they make fertile. And it is not, above all, autumn and the approaching fall of fruit whose seed they nourish that draws these tears from the wintry clouds. The pain is in summer itself, and death's bloom on the flower of life.

Just when the hour before noon comes to an end, as I go down into the valley full of the murmur of various fountains, I pause, enchanted by the chagrin. How bountiful are these waters! And if tears, like blood, are a constant wellspring within us, how fresh it is to listen to this liquid choir of voices rich and frail, and to match them with all the shades of our grief! There is no passion that can fail to lend you its tears, O fountains! And although I am content with the impact of a single drop that falls into the fountain from high above on the image of the moon, I will not in vain have learnt to know your haven through many afternoons, vale of sorrow.

Now, once more, I am in the plain. On the threshold of this hut where a candle for some rustic feast is lit in the inner darkness, a man sits with a dusty cymbal in his hand. The rain is pouring down; and alone, in the midst of the drenched solitude, I hear the squawk of a goose.

[January 1898]

Sailing by Night

I have forgotten why I undertook this voyage and what matter I was to negotiate, like Confucius when he brought his doctrine to the Prince of Wu. Sitting all day in the depths of my varnished cabin, my sense of urgency on these calm waters does not outpace the boat's swanlike progress. I go out at times only in the evening and sagely observe the features of the landscape.

This winter has no harshness. In a season dear to the philosopher, the bare trees and yellow grass are sufficient tokens of suspended time without the need for any superfluous awful cold and murderous violence to signal a definitive moment. In this twelfth month the country still spreads out, both funereal and productive, like a graveyard and a kitchen garden with mounds of tombs everywhere. The groves of blue bamboo, the dark pines on the graves, the sea-green reeds artfully hold and satisfy one's glance; and the yellow flowers of the New Year Candlestick and the berries of the Tallow Tree give an unpretentious air to the solemn picture. I sail in peace through this temperate region.

Now it is night. It would be useless to wait in the bow of my junk for our wooden anchor like a bait to draw the image of the waning moon over the blessed waters. Midnight alone will grant it to us. All is dark; but wherever the prow takes us on the pulse of the oar, there is no question of our losing our way. These channels have countless branches. Let us calmly pursue our journey with our eyes on that lone star.

[January 1898]

Halt on the Canal

Yet we go past the spot where the Old Man and Woman, driven by hunger from their distant village and guided by their tame duck on the raft they had made from their home door, realized they were entering a rich region by the appearance of waters that seemed to have had rice washed in them; we make our way, across the straight and wide canal bounded by the high rough wall that encloses the city and its people, to the place where the extended arch of a bridge frames the city gate's crenelated tower against the deep landscape; and we make fast our boat by placing a square stone in the grass among the tombs, like the obscure contribution of an epitaph.

And we begin our inquiry at daybreak, entering the endless corridor of the Chinese street like a dark wet trench smelling of innards, in the midst of a people intermingled with their houses like a bee with its wax and honey.

And for a long time we follow the narrow path in a hubbub like that of a fair. I see again a little girl unwinding a skein of green silk, a barber cleaning a customer's ear with a fine pincers like a lobster's antennae, a small donkey turning a millstone in the center of an oil merchant's warehouse, the dark calm of a pharmacy with the gold frame of a moon-shaped door at the back and two red tapers ablaze in front of the apothecary's name. We cross many courtyards, a hundred bridges; advancing along narrow alleys edged by sepia walls, we reach the wealthy quarter. If we were to go behind these closed doors, we would find vestibules flagged with stones, reception halls with wide bed-tables and small peach trees flowering in pots, smoky corridors with hams and boots hanging from the rafters. In ambush behind this wall, in a little courtyard, we discover the monstrous form of a prolific wisteria; its hundred creepers lace, intertwine, tie themselves in knots, become braided in a sort of twisted, misshapen cable that thrusts its long wooden snake in all directions and spreads over the trellis that covers the pit in a dense sky of mauve clusters. Let us cross the ruins of this long suburb where naked people are weaving silk among the debris. We reach the bare space that occupies the south side of the domain.

Here, they say, was once the imperial residence; and indeed the triple gate and quadruple jamb of successive doors bar the wide flagged path where we walk with their granite framework. But the enclosure in which we find ourselves contains nothing but rank grass; and at the crossroads of the "Four Ways" that lead off toward the four cardinal points, the imperial stele—a command and an inscription like a chart placed there for the entire realm—defaced by its fissured marble, bends over the headless tortoise it surmounts.

China everywhere presents the image of the constitutional void on which its system functions. "Let us," says the Tao-teh ching, "honor emptiness which gives the wheel its use and the lute its harmony." These ruins and fallow fields that one finds cheek by jowl with the densest multitudes, these barren mountains and endless expanses of graveyards next to the most painstaking tillage, do not convey a false idea; for in the mass and density of this coherent people, the administration, system of laws, religion, monarchy show a no less yawning vacuousness, empty images and their debris. Unlike Europe, China is not divided into compartments; no frontiers, no separate organisms within its immense surface have ever stemmed the spread of its throngs. And that is why this nation, as powerless as the ocean to foresee its own turmoils, is saved from destruction only by its flexibility: everywhere it shows an ancient, provisional character like nature itself—dilapidated, chancy, lacunal. The present always involves the reserves of the past and future. Men have not made a steady conquest of the land, a reasoned and definitive arrangement; the crowd still grazes on the grass.

And suddenly a lugubrious cry crushes us! For the guardian of the place, at the foot of one of the gates framing the countryside in the form of an upright letter, blows his long Chinese trumpet, and you see the thin brass pipe quivering with the energy of the breath that fills it. Raucous and muffled if the bell is turned to the ground, strident if it is raised, the noise, without inflexion or cadence, culminates in a melancholy brilliance on the beat of a terrible fourth: do fa, do fa! The abrupt cry of a peacock, in a similar way, underlines the forlorn nature of this drowsy garden. It is the shepherd's horn, not the bugle of statement and command; not the trumpet that leads armies with a song, rather an animal vociferation, and the horde or flock gather in confusion at its sound. But we are alone; and at this solemn crossroads the Mongol blows his trumpet for no living thing.

When we return to our boat, it is almost night. In the west the whole cloudy horizon seems dyed in blue, and on the dark land the fields of colza shine like flashes of light.

[April 1898]

The Pine Tree

The tree alone, in all of nature, is upright like a man for a symbolic reason.

A man stands erect by keeping his balance, and his two arms that hang at the ready at his sides are external to his unity. But the tree rises up with an effort; and, while it is held to the earth by the collective grasp of its roots, its manifold divergent parts, as they spread into the frail and sensitive tissue of leaves whereby it seeks its fulcrum in the air and light, are not only a gesture but an essential act and the condition of its stature.

The family of conifers has a special character. I see in them, not a ramification of the trunk by means of its branches, but their articulation on a stem that remains single and separate, and gradually loses its force among the threadlike leaves. The fir is a representative example; the essential plan of its symmetrical intersections is a right angle crossed by graded horizontals.

The species comprises many variations in different regions of the world. The most interesting is that of the pines I have studied in Japan.

Rather than the customary rigidity of the wood, the trunk here presents a fleshy elasticity. Under the tension of the rich fibrous cylinder it embraces, the sheath splits, and the rough bark, divided into pentagonal scales from which there oozes a plentiful resin, opens in strong layers. And if, by the suppleness of its apparently limp body, the stem yields to the external actions that violently attack or importune it, it resists by its own inherent energy; and the drama inscribed in the tormented system of its lines is the pathetic struggle of the tree.

So, along the tragic old road to Tokkaido, I saw the pines struggling in this manner with the powers of the air. Vainly do the ocean breezes press them down; clinging with all its roots to the stony soil, the unconquerable tree writhes, turns on itself, and like a man braced on the balanced four-fold system of his body, it faces up, kicks out in all directions, and seems to hold on to its adversary before finding its balance again and standing up under the various fierce attacks of the oppressive monster. One dark evening I reviewed their heroic lines of battle along the solemn beach and inspected all the outrages of fortune. One tree had fallen over backward and stretched to the sky a monstrous panoply of halberds and shields, which it brandished with a hundred fists; another, covered in wounds, mutilated as if it had been clubbed, and bristling on all sides with stumps and splinters, was still struggling and waving a few feeble boughs; still another seemed to resist the onslaught by turning its back and haunching down on the strong buttress of its straining thighs; finally, I saw giants and princes massively poised on their muscular loins who continued to hold their ground on all sides against their stormy adversary by the conjoined efforts of their Herculean arms.

I have still to speak of the leafage.

If I compare these pines to the species that thrive in loose earth and heavy rich soil, I find that the latter have four characteristics: the proportion of leaf to wood is greater; the leaf is deciduous; when flattened, it shows an obverse and reverse side; finally, the foliage on the boughs that diverge from a vertical line around a common center is arranged in a single bouquet. The pine, on the other hand, grows in dry stony soil; hence it absorbs the elements that nourish it in less immediate fashion and requires a fuller elaboration, a greater functional and, as it were, more personal activity. Obliged to absorb water in a measured way, it does not expand like a calix. The tree I observe divides its leaves, and spreads its young shoots on every side; instead of leaves to take in the rain, tufts of small tubes reach into the surrounding dampness and absorb it. And that is why the pine, independent of the seasons and sensitive to more constant and more subtle influences, has evergreen foliage.

I have, then, explained the character of this foliage—aerial, suspended, fragmentary. Just as the pine lends the fanciful framework of its boughs to a harmonious landscape and thus enhances nature's charm and splendor, so it casts the form of its singular tufts over all things: over the force and glory of the Ocean, blue in the sun; over the harvests; and over the sky, interrupting the designs of the constellations or the dawn. It bends its terraces under azalea bushes that flame as far as the gentian blue lakes, or above the steep walls of the imperial city as far as the silver and grass-green canals. And on the evening I saw Fuji, like a colossus and a virgin enthroned in the brightness of the infinite, the dark tuft of a pine stood by the dove-colored mountain.

[June 1898]

The Golden Ark in the Forest

When I left Yeddo, the great sun was flaming in a clear sky. At afternoon's end, reaching the Utsunomiya junction, I saw the clouds darkening all of the west. Composed of huge cumuli, they had the voluminous and chaotic appearance you sometimes find of an evening when low light on the horizon, like veiled footlights, casts shadows back over the fields of clouds and brings out the contrasts in reverse fashion. On the platform, in one drowsy moment, and for a long while afterward in the train that took me west, I was the spectator of the day's decline and the gradual massing of the clouds. In a glance, I grasped the lie of the land: far off in the distance, dark forests and the folds of heavy mountains; in the foreground, detached buttresses barring the way one after another like a series of parallel screens. The trenches we followed showed us the earth's layers: first, thin humus as black as coal, then yellow sand, finally clay red with sulphur or cinnabar. Avernus opened and spread before us. Do not the burnt earth, low sky, bitter circle of volcanoes and fir trees correspond to the black abyss from which our dream visions arise? So, with royal wisdom, the ancient shogun Ieyasu chose this place to lay its shadows over the shade to which he was returning, and dissolving his silence in their opaqueness, to transmute his dead person into a godhead by the affinity of temple with tomb.

The forest of clyptomeria is truly this temple.

Yesterday, in the somber twilight, I already crossed several times the double avenue of giant trees that leads the annual ambassador bearing the imperial gifts for the kingly ancestor from twenty leagues away to the red bridge. But this morning, when the first rays of the sun were turning the banks of dark greenery above me to pink in the golden breeze, I went into the colossal nave, deliciously full of nocturnal cold and the smell of resin.

The clyptomeria belongs to the family of pines, and the Japanese call it *sagui*. It is a very tall tree whose trunk, without bends or knots, observes a strict rectitude. You do not see branches but occasional clumps of leaves which, in the way of pines, are not indicated by mass and contrast but blob and outline, and float like wisps of black smoke about the mystic pillar; and at the same height the forest of straight trunks vanishes in the tangled canopy and shadows of inextricable foliage. The place is at once limitless and closed, prepared and empty.

The marvelous Houses are scattered in the woods.

I shall not describe the entire system of the shadowy City as its plan, in minute detail, is recorded on my fan. In the midst of the monumental forest I followed the avenues barred by scarlet *torii*. At a bronze basin, under a roof brought back from the moon, I filled my mouth with lustral waters; I climbed the stairways; among the crowd of pilgrims, I crossed something rich and open on all sides, a gate in the center of the enclosure like the dream of a confused mass of flowers and birds; barefoot, I went into the golden interior; I saw priests with haughty faces, their heads crested with horsehair, and wearing wide green silk trousers, who made the morning sacrifice to the sounds of flute and mouth-organ. And the sacred *kagura* on his platform, his countenance framed by a white cap, and devoutly holding in his hands the golden tuft, the tasseled bough, performed the dance of continuous departures and returns.

In China the basic architectural element is the baldachin, with its sides raised on pikes of the pastoral tent. But in Japan the roofs, whether of tiles or bark—the latter, strong and light, resembling thick felt—show only a slight curve at the corners: in their elegant strength they are just lids, and everything here evolves from the idea of a box. From the time Jingo Tenno with his fleet conquered the islands of the Rising Sun, the Japanese have in all places preserved the sign of the sea. The habit of tucking up their clothes to the loins, the low cabins in which they live on an unsteady soil, the skillfully made multitude of small objects that they carefully stow away, the absence of furniture—do not all things, in sum, point to a sailor's confined life on the insecure plank of his ship? And these wooden houses I see are but the enlarged cabin of a galley, the box of a palanquin. In similar fashion, the crossed extensions of the frames, the oblique shafts from which figured heads jut out at the four angles—they too recall the portable nature of the whole. Among the temple columns, they are arks that have been set down.

Houses, yes. Here the sanctuary is properly a house. Higher up the mountain slope, the bones have been put in a bronze cylinder. But in this room, seated on his unalterable name, the dead man's soul continues a spectral existence in the darkness of the closed splendor.

Contrary to the practice that uses and valorizes stone and wood in accordance with their intrinsic virtues and without the admixture of foreign elements, the artful skill here consists of reducing matter to naught. The compartments, sides of boxes, parqueted floors and ceilings, no longer made of beams and boards, are a manner of opaque exorcism of images. Color dresses, decorates the wood; lacquer drowns it beneath impenetrable waters; paint veils it under marvels; sculpture deeply erodes and transfigures it. The tops of partitions, the smallest spikes are covered with arabesques and checkered patterns as soon as they come to the magic surface. But as on screens you see the mountains and the trees in bloom steeped in a radiant mist, so these palaces emerge entirely from gold. On the roofs, on the façades lit by the full light of day, only the ridges are burnished with scattered brightness, yet vast surfaces of the side buildings gleam through the shadows; and inside, the six walls of the box are painted alike with the splendor of the hidden treasure, the absent torch revealed in changeless mirrors.

Thus the magnificent shogun does not inhabit a wooden house; but his dwelling in the heart of the forest is the evening's declining glory; and an ambrosial haze abides under the level boughs.

Through the huge valley of this region filled like a god's slumbers with an ocean of trees, the dazzling waterfall here and there bursts from the foliage, which blends with the multiple murmur.

[June 1898]

The Wanderer

In June, with a crooked stick in my hand like the god Bishamon, I am that strange passerby who meets a naïve band of ruddy-faced peasant girls; and, in the evening, at six o'clock, while the storm cloud endlessly pursues its monotonous assault on the mountain, that lone man on the dilapidated road. I have not gone anywhere, my wanderings are without profit or aim; the journeys of the soldier and the merchant, the pilgrimage of the sterile woman who goes around the holy mountain seven times in humble hope, do not resemble my circuit. The familiar path does not appeal to me until it leads me astray and soon, embarrassed by the secret that a black camelia leaf confides to the moss in the depths of the woods with a hushed tear, I suddenly run off like an awkward deer and, poised on one foot, listen for the echo in the leafy solitude. How fresh and comic the small bird's song seems to me! And what pleasure I take in the distant cry of the rooks! Every tree has its personality, every small beast its role, every voice its part in the symphony. As one says one understands music, so I *understand* nature, like a detailed narrative of proper names; and as my walk and the day advance, so does the elaboration of the doctrine. Once, with delight, I discovered that all things exist in a certain accord, and now my glance alone confirms the secret relationship by which the black of this pine marries the bright green of the maples over there; and, reinstating the original design, I call my visit a revision. I am the Inspector of Creation, the Verifier of things present; the world's solidity is the matter of my beatitude! At ordinary times we use things for a purpose and forget the pure fact that they *are*; but when, after long effort, parting the brambles and branches, I penetrate historically into the heart of the glade and place my hand on the burning rump of this massive rock, Alexander's entrance into Jerusalem is like the hugeness of my recognition.

And I walk on and on! All of us embrace the autonomous principle of our mobility by which we advance to our food and work. For me, the even movement of my legs allows me to gauge the force of more subtle appeals. I feel the attraction of all things in the silence of my soul.

I understand the world's harmony. When will I grasp its melody?

[June 1898]

Here and There

In Nihon Bashi Street, near the booksellers and vendors of lanterns, embroideries, and bronzes, plots of land are sold retail; and as an attentive window-shopper of this fanciful display, I haggle with myself over the price of fragments of the world. The artists have subtly made themselves masters of the exquisite laws by which the features of the landscape are composed like those of a face: instead of copying nature, they imitate it, building their counterfeits in the way a rule is shown by an example as exact as the eyes can make them yet miniature like an image. All the different kinds of pine trees, for instance, are there for me to choose from; and they express in proportionate terms by their positions in the jars the amount of space appropriate to their size. Here is the ricefield in spring; in the distance, the hill fringed with trees (they are moss). Here is the sea with its archipelagoes and capes; by the artifice of two stones, one black, the other red and seemingly worn and porous, two islands are joined by the perspective adopted, their varied distances being brought out only by their different colors in the setting sun. Even the iridescence of the many-colored waters is captured by this bed of motley pebbles covered by the contents of two carafes.

—Now, to develop my thought.

The European artist *copies* nature in accordance with his feeling for it, the Japanese *imitates* it in accordance with the means he borrows from it. The former expresses himself, the latter expresses nature; one fashions, the other mimicks; one paints, the other composes; one is a student, the other, in a way, a *master*; one reproduces in detail the spectacle he sees with an honest and subtle glance, the other extracts from it the law in the wink of an eye and applies it with scriptural brevity, in the freedom of his fancy.

Here the artist's initial inspiration is the matter on which he exercises his hand. Cheerfully he considers the intrinsic virtues, the shades, and having appropriated the soul of the brute thing, makes himself its interpreter. Of the entire story he extracts from it, he tells only the essential and significant points, just giving a few fleeting indications here and there and leaving to the paper alone the task of concealing all the endless complexity that is implied, more than hinted, by a charming brushstroke. It is play in certainty, caprice in necessity; and the idea, wholly captured in the argument, imposes itself on us with cunning precision.

To speak first of the colors: we see that the Japanese artist has reduced his palette to a small number of general, predetermined tones. He has understood that the beauty of a color resides less in its intrinsic quality than its implicit harmony with related tones: and, since the relationship between two values, when augmented in even quantity, is not modified, he repairs the omission of all neutral and varied tones by the liveliness he gives to the combination of the essential notes, soberly indicating one or two responses. He knows that the value of a tone depends on its position rather than its intention, and, master of the keys, transposes them at will. And as color is but the particular tribute that all things visible pay to universal light, everything takes its place in the frame by virtue of light, and in accordance with the theme chosen by the artist.

But the eye that has been blinking now concentrates its gaze and, instead of contemplating, questions. Color is one of matter's passions, it denotes the participation of each object in the common source of glory; while drawing expresses the energy proper to each being, its action, rhythm, dance. The former shows position in space, the latter fixes movement in time. One gives form, the other meaning. And as the Japanese artist, careless of relief, paints only by contour and blob, the basic element of his drawing is a diagrammatic stroke. The tones are juxtaposed, the lines join; and as painting is a harmony, drawing is a concept. If the knowledge one has of anything is just an insight, immediate, whole, and simultaneous, drawing is like a word made of letters and gives an abstract, efficient meaning, and a pure idea. Each form, movement, group provides its hieroglyph.

And that is what I understand when I plunge into the bundles of

Japanese prints. Likewise, at Shizuoka, among the ex-votos of the temple, I saw many admirable examples of the same art. A swarthy warrior springs from the worm-eaten wood like a frenzied interjection; this rearing, kicking thing is no longer the image of a horse but the ciphered thought of its leap; and a sort of reversed and enhanced six with a mane and tail figures its repose in the grass. Embraces, battles, landscapes, crowds, inserted in a small space, are like the seals of a document. This man bursts out laughing and, falling over, one no longer knows whether he is still a man or already an inscription, his own graphic symbol.

—The horrid French or English build their shacks barbarously, crudely, anywhere, without pity for the earth they disfigure, concerned only to possess the largest possible space with their gaze, if not their greedy hands. They exploit a view as they would a waterfall. The Oriental knows to flee the vast landscapes whose multiple aspects and diverging lines do not lend themselves to the exquisite accord of eye and view that alone makes a place necessary. His home is not open to all the winds; his concern is to achieve a perfect retreat in the nook of some peaceful valley where his glance is so indispensable to the harmony of the picture he sees before him that he is unable to do without it. His eyes give him all he needs for his well-being, and he replaces furniture by his open window. Inside, the art of the painter ingeniously calques his visions on the fictitious transparency of the frame, multiplying imaginary openings. In the old imperial palace I visited, all the magnificent, imponderable features have been taken away, leaving only the painted decoration, the familiar field of vision of its august inhabitant installed there as in a camera obscura. The paper apartment is composed of successive compartments divided by partitions that slide on grooves. For each series of rooms a single decorative theme has been chosen and introduced by a play of screens like the wooden uprights of a theatrical decor; thus at my ease I can lengthen or shorten my gaze. I am less the beholder of these paintings than their host. And each theme is expressed by the choice of a uniform color in harmony with the paper's intrinsic tone, and marking the opposite end of the gamut. Thus at Gosho the cream and indigo motif is sufficient for the "Freshness-and-Purity" apartment to seem replete with sky and water. But at Nijo the Imperial dwelling place is of gold alone. Emerging from the mat-covered floor that abbreviates them, crowns of pine trees unfold their monstrous arms on the sunny walls, painted life-size. The prince, when seated, saw before him, and on his right and left, nothing but great bands of tawny fire; and he felt himself floating on evening and holding its solemn furnace beneath him.

—At Shizuoka, in the Rinzaiji temple, I saw a landscape made of colored dust. It had been put under glass for fear a breath of air might blow it away.

—Time is measured there among the leaves, in front of the golden Buddha, by the burning of a small candle and, in the depths of this ravine, by the flow of a triple fountain.

—Tumbling, swept off his feet in the chaotic hurly-burly of the unfathomable sea, lost in the plashing abyss, mortal man seeks with all his strength something solid to which to cling. That is why he adds the human face to the permanence of wood, metal, or stone, and makes it the object of his devotion and prayer. He gives proper names, as well as common ones, to natural forces and, by means of the concrete image that designates them like a vocable, humiliated yet still strangely aware of the higher authority of the Word, he invokes them in his hour of need. Rather like a little girl who makes up the story of her doll from bits and pieces of everything, humanity found the way to enrich its mythological novel by memory and dreams. And here beside me is this poor little old woman who, as she earnestly claps her hands, makes her salutation before the female colossus in whose bosom an ancient Prince, warned by toothache and a dream to honor his former skull, implanted here its wasted bubble when he found it caught in the roots of a willow tree. To my right and left, for the whole length of the dark shed, the three thousand golden Kwannons, all identical, in the decor of arms that frame them, are lined up fifteen deep in files of one hundred; a ray of light makes this divine rubbish dump swarm. And if I wish to know why the crowd is uniform, or from what bulb all these identical stalks have sprung, I find that the worshiper here seeks a greater surface to echo his prayer, and fancies he is multiplying its efficacy by the number of objects.

But the sages did not long limit their gaze to the gaze of these brute images; and, having realized the coherence of all things, they made this one fact the basis of their philosophy. For if each thing was individually precarious and transitory, the richness of the whole was inexhaustible. There was no need for a man to apply an axe to a tree, a chisel to a rock: in the millet seed and the egg, as in the calm and turmoil of the land and sea, they found the same principle of plastic energy; and the earth was sufficient for the making of its own idols. And holding that everything is constituted of homogeneous parts, then training their analysis on themselves the better to pursue their thought, they discovered that the fleeting, unprovable, unjustifiable thing in themselves was the fact of their presence in the place they found themselves, as elements freed from space and time: the very concept of their own contingency.

And if a devilish fraud had not led them astray at this point, they would have recognized a practice analogous to that of speech in the relationship between a principle of existence, independent with respect to its proper notion of everything and its precarious expression; implying assent, or the intelligible restitution of breath. For each creature, born of the impress of divine unity on indeterminate matter, *is* the very assent that the creature *gives* its creator, and the *expression* of the Nothingness from which its creator drew it. Such is the vital respiratory rhythm of the world of which man, endowed with consciousness and speech, was appointed the priest, to make dedication and offering of it as well as of his own nothingness conjoined with essential grace, by the filial gift of himself and a loving, conjugal preference.

But their blinded eyes refused to recognize unconditional being, and it was given to him named Buddha to perfect the pagan blasphemy. To take up again the comparison with speech: from the moment they ignored the object of speech, order and sequence escaped them, and they found only garrulous delirium. Yet man bears within him the horror of that which is not the Absolute, and you did not hesitate, Buddha, to embrace Nothingness in order to break the awful circle of Vanity. For, as he sought an intrinsic principle in the thing itself instead of explaining everything by an external end, he found only Nothingness, and his doctrine taught a monstrous communion. The method is for the sage finally to reach Nothingness, having nullified in his mind each after each the idea of form, and pure space, and the very idea of the idea, and *then* to enter Nirvana. As for me, I find here the idea of Nothingness added to that of *enjoyment*. This is the ultimate Satanic mystery, the silence of the creature retrenched in a total refusal, the incestuous quietude of the soul seated on its own essential difference.

[June 1898]

The Sedentary

I live on the top story, and at the very corner, of a square, spacious home. I have put my bed in the embrasure of the window and, when evening comes, like the spouse of a god who silently climbs onto the bed, I lie down naked at full length with my face to the night. At a certain moment, raising an eyelid heavy as by death, my glance merges with a rose-colored brightness. But now, again emerging with a groan from a sleep like that of the first man, I wake in the vision of gold. The mosquito net's frail tissue shivers in an ineffable breath of air. Here is light itself purged of heat; and, twisting slowly in the delicious cold, if I extend my bare arm I can thrust it up to the shoulder into the substance of this glory, plunge it and feel with my hand the fountain of eternity like the trembling waters of a spring. I see the magnificent estuary irresistibly rise from the depths to the apex of the sky like a clear, concave basin the color of mulberry leaves. Only the face of the sun and its unbearable fires, only the deadly force of its darts, will drive me from my bed. I foresee that I shall need to spend the day in fasting and solitude. What water will be pure enough to slake my thirst? What fruit shall I peel with a golden knife to satisfy my heart?

But after the sun has reached its zenith followed like a shepherd by the sea and by the crowds of mortals that rise in successive ranks, it is Noon, and everything that has dimension in space is enveloped by the soul of fire itself, whiter than a thunderbolt. The world is erased, the seals of the furnace are broken; all things have vanished in the bosom of this new flood. I have closed all the windows. Prisoner of light, I keep the diary of my captivity. And at times, with my hand on the paper, I write in the same way as the silkworm that spins its thread from the leaf it devours; at other times I wander through the shadowy rooms, from the dining room, through the parlour, where I rest my hand for a moment on the lid of the organ, to this bare room whose center is occupied by the solitary, fearsome worktable. And inside white lines on the paper that mark the breaches in my hermetic prison, I bring to ripeness the idea of a holocaust. Ah, if it is desirable to be dissolved in the flaming embrace, to be carried off in the raging whirlwind, how much more beautiful is the torture of a mind devoured by light!

And when the afternoon is filled with the ardent sweetness that precedes evening like the feeling of paternal love, I return to the topmost bedroom, having purified body and mind. And taking up an inexhaustible book I pursue the study of Being, the distinctions of person and substance, of qualities and predicaments. Between the two rows of houses, the vision of a river closes my street; its enormous silver flood is smoking, and great white-sailed ships cross the shining gap with a smooth, proud grace. And I see before me the very "River of Life," the metaphor of which I borrowed as a child from the discourses on morality. But today, though a stubborn swimmer, I no longer cherish the hope of coming ashore among the reeds face down in the silt of the further shore. Under the salutation of palms, in a silence broken by the squeal of a parrot, let the thin cascade invite me as it beats on the gravel behind the fleshy leafage of the magnolia; let the fabled bough bend under the weight of the myrobalans and pomegranates. Tearing my eyes away from an angelic science, I shall no longer consider the garden that is offered for my future delight and recreation.

[June 1898]

The Land Viewed from the Sea

Coming from the horizon, our ship is met by the world's pier, and the unsubmerged planet unfolds its huge architecture before us. When I climb to the bridge I see the blue spectacle of the land adorned in the morning light with a great star. The Continent has established the deep bulwark of its fortifications to shield the Sun from the Ocean's restless pursuit. The breaches open to a happy countryside.

And for a long while, in the day's full light, we skirt the boundary of the other world. Carried by the breath of the trade wind, our ship speeds and bounds on the elastic depths where it leans with all its weight. I am caught in blue, stuck like a barrel: captive of boundlessness, hanging from the Sky's intersection, I see the entire dark Earth laid out before me like a map—the huge, humble World. This separation is beyond cure: all things are far from me, and sight alone binds me to them. I shall not be allowed to build a house of wood and stone with my hands, nor peaceably to eat the meals cooked on a domestic fire. Soon we shall turn our prow back toward that which has no shore and, beneath a formidable spread of sails, proceed in the midst of monstrous eternity, our way now marked only by our sidelights.

[September 1898]

Salutation

And once more I salute this land like the lands of Gessen and Canaan. Last night, when our ship was tossing at the river entrance in the wheat-colored moonlight, what a sign low in the sky, on the other side of the waters, did the "Dog" Lighthouse make to me, standing like a golden watchman at the foot of the starry expanse, an oil-fired splendor on the earth's horizon. But smooth waters have brought us into the heart of the region, and I disembark; and on my way I see below me the image of the round sun repeated over and again in the depths of the fields, red in the green rice.

It is neither cold nor too hot: all of nature has the heat of my body. How the feeble chirp of the crickets beneath the grass touches me! At the season's end, in this testamentary moment, the union of sky and earth, less sacramental today than amorous, consummates a nuptial solemnity. O harsh fate! Is there no rest but where I am not? Is there no peace for the heart of man? A spirit born for enjoyment alone brooks no delay. Possession itself at some future time will not dry my tears; no joy of mine will be enough to obliterate the bitterness of reparation.

And I shall not salute this land with a shallow cast of invented words; but let me suddenly find in myself a large discourse that compasses the foot of the hills like a sea of corn crossed by a triple river. I fill the space between the mountains like a plain and its roads. With both eyes lifted to the everlasting hills, I salute the earth's venerable body in the name of all things. I no longer see outward trappings in the air but very substance, the giant assemblage of members. O edges of the cup all about me! It is by you that we receive the waters of the sky, and you are the recipient of the offering! This damp morning, at the bend of the road between the tomb and the tree, I saw the massive dark slope, barred at its foot by the dazzling line of the river, that rose in noon's light like a stream of milk.

And like a body that sinks of its own weight into water, I have advanced for these four still hours in the bosom of light, feeling a divine resistance. I stand in the midst of the perfectly white air. I celebrate the orgy of ripeness with a shadowless body. It is no longer the hungry sun beneath whose strength the torn, sweaty land suddenly bursts and violently blooms. Lustral moment! A constant current of air blows on us from between east and north. The rich harvest, the trees heavy with their fruit, endlessly stir in a breeze both strong and light. The earth's fruits are blown back and forth in the purifying brightness. The sky is no more far above us; having wholly descended, it submerges and drenches us. Like Hylas, who saw horizontal fish hanging above him in a glassy space, I see a dazzling white bird with a pink throat that bursts forth from this milk, this silver in which I drown, and again is lost in a glow my eyes cannot sustain.

And the entire day shall not exhaust my salutation. At the dark hour when the nuptial procession armed with flaming torches leads the groom's chair through the forest of orange trees, applause and acclamation from my whole being rise above the smoking mountains to the red sign I see. I salute the threshold, the brute evidence of hope, the reward of man uncompromised; I raise my hands to this display of a manly color! Autumnal victor, the leafage above my head is mingled with small oranges. Yet once more in the world of men, I must show this face of mine lifted from childhood toward Death, like a singer with his heart lost to the beat and his eye on the score who waits with parted lips to join in.

[October 1898]

The Suspended House

By an underground stairway I go down to the suspended house. As the swallow builds the shelter of its patience between plank and rafter, as the seagull glues its nest like a blanket to the rock, so, by a system of clamps, trusses and beams set deep in the stone, the box where I live holds fast to the vault of the huge porch dug into the mountain. A trap in the floor of the inner room brings me home comforts: every second day I drop my small panier at the end of a rope, and reel it up filled with a little rice, roasted pistachios, and vegetables pickled in brine. In a corner of the fearsome cliff, like a trophy made from the Parca's scalp, hangs a fount whose endless weeping is carried away by the chasm. I get the water I need by a rope knotted between the clear tufts, and the smell of my cooking mingles with the plashing cascade. The torrent vanishes among the palms, and I see below me the tall trees that furnish the ritual perfumes. And as a broken wine glass is enough to shatter the night, and as the hollow, neutral tinkling of endless rain on a deep stone wakens the whole world's keyboard, so I see the monstrous funnel where I nest as the very auricle of this massive rock, like an ear gouged in a stone temple; and with my attention focused on every articulation of my body, I try to feel, above the noise of the birds and leaves, that which this enormous secret pavilion no doubt implies: the tides of universal waters, the flexions of geological strata, the groans of the earth as it wheels under the diverse tensions of gravity. Once a year the moon rises over the escarpment on my left and cuts the shadow at waist-height, at so exact a level that with great precaution and care I can float a copper plate on it. But most of all I love the last step of the stairway that goes down into the void. How often have I woken from my meditations, bathed in night's tears like a rosebush, or on idle afternoons thrown handfuls of dry lichees, like small red bells, to the monkeys perched on the topmost branches below me.

[October 1898]

The Spring

The crow, focusing one eye on me like a clockmaker on his watch, would see me, a precise miniature being, my walking stick held like a dart in my hand, advancing along the narrow path with an exact movement of my legs. The landscape within the circle of enclosing mountains is as flat as a pan. On my right and left the vast activity of the harvest is underway; the earth is being shorn like a lamb. I fight for the width of the path and my footing on it with the endless line of workers going to the fields, their billhooks at their waists, and with those returning, bent like scales under their loaded double baskets, their forms both round and square marrying the symbols of earth and sky. I walk for a long time: the expanse is enclosed like a room, the air dark, and long columns of motionless smoke hover above us like the remnants of some barbaric funeral pyre. I leave the cropped fields and muddy harvests, and little by little enter the narrowing gorge. After the fields of sugarcane come the hollow reeds; and three times, with my shoes in my hands, I cross the swift waters gathered in the body of a stream. Here where the river is born of the depths of a five-gorged valley, I set out to find the source of one of the streamlets that feed it. The climb grows steeper as the thread of the cascade lessens. I leave the last fields of sweet potatoes beneath me.

And suddenly I have come into a wood like the wood of Parnassus, which served the assemblies of the Muses! Around me, tea-trees lift their twisted shoots and dark sharp-edged foliage so high my hand at full stretch cannot reach inside. Lovely retreat! Strange, artful shades decked with a perennial bloom! Subtle perfume that seems to linger rather than emanate, and pleases the nostrils as it revives the spirit. And in a hollow I find the spring. Like grain from a furious hopper, water spurts from underneath the earth in fits and starts. Corruption absorbs; only that which is pure, originary, immediate bursts forth. Born of the sky's dew, gathered in some deep matrix, the deep virginal waters issue forth with mighty force like a shout. Happy are they from whom a new word violently bursts! Let my mouth be like that of this spring forever full, born here of its own simple everlasting birth, careless of serving the labors of men and of the lowlands, where it will spread out and mix like saliva with the mud, nourishing the huge, still harvest.

[November 1898]

Noon Tide

When the time comes for him to sail no longer, the sailor makes his home by the shore; and when the sea moans, unable to go back to sleep, he gets up to keep watch, like a nurse who hears a child whimpering in the night. I do the same, and, by the living virtue of the liquid that pervades me, my mind communicates with the movement of the waters in the manner of a city with its hidden sewers. While I am speaking, or writing, or resting, or eating, I am at one with the sea as it rises and retreats. And often at noon, as the short-term citizen of this merchant shore, I come to see what the tide, the ocean's lunar oscillation, has brought us, and changed by this river trough into a wide current of yellow water.

And I attend to the mounting toward me of all the people of the sea, the solemn procession of ships drawn by the tide as by a tow chain: the wide-bellied junks with their four lopsided sails in the wind as stiff as shovels; those from Foochow with huge faggots of beams lashed to each side; then tricolored sampans, the giants of Europe, the American windjammers full of kerosene, all the camels of Madian, the cargo boats of Hamburg and London, the traders of the coast and the islands. Everything is limpid; I enter a brightness so pure it seems that neither my intimate consciousness, nor my body, offers any resistance. The weather is deliciously cold. With my mouth shut and my nostrils given to the exhilarating air, I breathe the sun.

But when noon sounds at the Customs tower, the semaphore ball falls and all the boats strike the hour, the cannon thunders, somewhere the Angelus tolls, the factory whistle mingles for a long time with the sirens' blare. All of humanity gathers to eat. The sampan man, at the stern of his barge, raising the wooden lid, watches with contented eyes as his stew comes to the boil; the tall coolies who do the unloading, packaged in thick rags and with shoulder pieces like pikes, besiege the open-air kitchens; while those who have already been served sit laughing with a bowl of steaming rice in both hands and test the heat with the greedy tips of their tongues. The governor-valve rises; all the plugs of the earth are satisfied; the rivers suspend their course, and the sea, as it meets them, mixing its salt with their sand, comes whole and entire to drink at their mouths. It is the time of plenty. Now the winding canals that cross the city are one long snake of linked barges that proceed in the hue and cry; and the swell of irresistible waters raises the pontoons and moorings and buoys them like corks.

[December 1898]

Peril of the Sea

As we cannot eat, I go up again to the poop with a chunk of bread in my pocket; and staggering, deafened, slapped in the face, I rejoin the wild shadows and massive din of the roiling storm. I open my lips in this void and blindly take a mouthful to them. Soon, however, I leave the binnacle's glow and, as my eyes little by little grow used to the darkness, they recognize the form of the ship and, beyond it, the elemental sea in the clutches of the wind as far as the near horizon. I see the pale cavalry of foam charging in the black circle. Nothing around me is solid; I stand in chaos; I am lost in the belly of Death. My heart is torn by the chagrin of the last hour. This is no threat brandished at me: I have simply intruded on the uninhabitable, I am out of my depth, I travel in the midst of indifference. I am at the mercy of the onslaught of the ocean depths and wind, the powers of Emptiness. There is no pact with the upheaval around me, and the handful of souls held by this narrow vessel would dissolve in liquid matter like a basket of bran. On the bosom of the Abyss about to engulf me, encompassed by the complicity of my own weight, I am held in a frail equation. Yet I return to my cabin and go to bed, anxious to escape this vision of sadness. The ship, with its prow to the wind, rises to the waves, and at times the huge machine, with its iron plate and boilers, its armament and holds filled chockablock with coal and projectiles, squats down on the waves as far as it can like a horsewoman crouching over her shins to take a jump. Then comes a brief calm, and I hear far below the screw as it pursues its frail, homely noise.

But before the next day is over our ship enters this isolated port closed by its mountain like a dam. Here once more is life! Touched with rustic joy, I again take up my interrupted survey of the dense and fervent enterprise of common riches that is life, the assiduous, multiple, complex action by which all things exist together. Just as we drop anchor, the sun, through clefts in the mountain that hides it, casts on the earth four fiery jets so strong they seem to be emissions of its very substance. Upright on the topmost ridge, the King, before raising his light vertically to the boundless sky—Eye of our eyes—in the merciful expansion of Vision visible, makes a majestic display of distance and origin at this supreme hour. I am greeted by a farewell richer than a promise! The mountain has put on its hyacinth robe, the violet marriage of gold and night. I am overcome by a deep, mighty joy. I raise my thanks to God to be still alive, and my whole being expands to gauge my reprieve.

This time, yet again, I shall not drink the bitter waters.

[January 1899]

A Proposition on Light

I cannot believe—indeed, everything in me wholly rejects the belief—
that colors are the primary element and that light is but the synthesis of
their septenary. I do not see that light is white, nor that any color affects
its intrinsic virtue, nor that a harmony of colors determines it. There is
no color without an extrinsic support; hence we know that color itself
is an exterior thing, the varied testimony that matter pays to the single
source of indivisible splendor. Do not pretend to decompose light, for
it is light that decomposes darkness, producing seven notes according
to the intensity of its efforts. A vase full of water or a prism allow us to
see this in action by the intrusion of a dense transparent medium and
the refractive play of facets. The free direct beam of light remains un-
changed; color appears as soon as refractions are captured, that is, as
soon as matter assumes its special function. The prism embraces all the
possible play of reflexions in the calculated space of its three angles and
the concerted action of its triple dihedral mirror, giving back to light its
color equivalent. I compare light to a woven fabric, its rays constituting
the warp, its wave of color (always implying a reverberation) the woof.
Color involves only the woof.

If I examine a rainbow or the spectrum projected on a wall, I see a
gradation both of the nature of the hues and of their relative intensity.
Yellow occupies the center of the iris, pervading it to its outer edges
that, as they grow darker, gradually exclude it. We can perceive it to be
the most immediate veil of light, whereas red and blue are its reciprocal
images, a balanced two-termed metaphor. Yellow plays the role of me-
diator: blending with the neighboring bands, it prepares the mixed
tones and, by them, calls forth the complementary colors. In and by
way of yellow, extreme red combined with green, just as blue combined
with orange, vanish in the unity of whiteness.

Color is thus a particular phenomenon of reflexion in which the re-
flecting body, penetrated by light, appropriates light to itself and re-
stores it in altered form; it is the result of the analysis and examination
of all things by the ray that cannot be denied. And the intensity of tones

varies in accordance with a gamut whose keynote is yellow, and in relation to the greater or lesser complete response of matter to the sollicitations of light. Who cannot but be shocked by the postulate of classical theory according to which the hue of an object results from its absorption of all the colored rays except the one it exhibits? I am led to believe, on the contrary, that the visible individuality of each thing is an original, authentic quality, and that color, no less than perfume, is a property of the rose.

—What has been measured is not the speed of light, but simply the resistance that the environment makes to light as it transforms it.

—And visibility itself is only one of the properties of light that differ according to different subjects.

[1899]

Hours in the Garden

There are people whose eyes alone are sensitive to light; and what for most of them is the sun but a cost-free lantern by whose light each comfortably carries out the work of his or her particular estate, the writer with his pen, the farmer with his ox? But I absorb light with my eyes and ears, and my mouth and nose, and all the pores of my skin. I soak in it like a fish, I swallow it. As they say that the fires of morning and afternoon ripen wine in the bottles exposed to them, like grapes once more on the vine, so the sun permeates my blood and makes my brain laugh. Let us enjoy this calm, burning hour. I am like the seaweed in the current held by its foot alone, its density equal to the water, or like the Australian palm with its high crest perched on a long mast and wide beating wings all bathed in evening gold, as it bends, rolls, and springs back on the spread and balance of its vast, supple fronds.

—The formidable aloe doubtless sprang from one of the teeth sown by Cadmus in the ploughed Theban field. The sun drew this warrior from a fierce soil. It is a heart of swords, a bloom of glaucous straps. The sentinel of loneliness, sea-colored, armour-colored, it traverses the artichoke on all sides with its huge saws. And for a long time in this way it will raise its harrows rank upon rank until it dies after blooming, and its floral member bursts from its heart like a post and a candelabra and a banner rooted in the entrails of the last squad of warriors!

—By my order the door has been bolted and barred. The porter sleeps in his recess, his head slumped on his breast; all the servants are asleep. A single pane of glass separates me from the garden, and the silence is so exquisite that everything—even the walls of the enclosure, the mice between the floorboards, the lice in the pigeon's breasts, the bubble of a dandelion on its fragile roots—must feel the pivotal noise of the door I open. In the afternoon brightness I see the expanse of sky and the sun in the place I had imagined. A hawk is hovering in wide circles in the blue; a bird dropping falls from the crest of a pine. I am happy where I am. My movements in this closed space are marked by caution and calm vigilance, like the fisherman who fears to ruffle the water and the fish if he so much as thinks. Nothing recalls a free open countryside that diverts the mind and leads the body astray. Trees and flowers conspire in my captivity, and the path's cochlear fold over and again brings me back to some focal point, indicated, as in the game of goose, by the well in the most secret corner. I shake the unseen bucket, contrived through the entire thickness of the hill, by means of the rope that serves as axis for the long bottleneck of the opening. In the stillness, like a fruit and like a poet ripening his sugar, I touch that within which life is measured out to us by the circulation of the sun, the pulse of my four limbs, and the growth of my hair. Vainly the turtledove makes her pure sad call in the distance. I shall not budge today. In vain the deep murmur of the swollen river reaches me.

—At midnight, returning from a ball where for several hours I watched human bodies, some in black sheaths, others in strange flags, revolving two by two (each face expressing an incomprehensible satisfaction) to the gymnastic modulations of a piano, I see by the light of my lantern, in the torrential downpour, just when the porters have lifted me to the top of the stairway and raised the curtain of my litter— the magnolia wholly decked with its great ivory lamps. Oh, fresh apparition! Proof of unfailing treasure in the night!

—The theme of the earth is expressed by the detonations of that far-off drum, like a cooper you hear in a deep cellar striking the casks with measured beat. The world's magnificence is such that one expects at any moment to find the silence shattered by the frightful explosion of a cry, the *ta-ra-ba* of a trumpet, the delirious exultation, the drunken elucidation of the brass! The news spreads that the rivers have reversed their course and as the flooding streams are further swollen by the growing surge, all the small sea craft go down into the hinterland to trade the horizon's produce. The work of the fields profits from the change: the chain-pumps turn and chat with each other, and all space is filled with a hydraulic noise until the hour when the drenched harvest, mingling with the dark prairie, mirrors the guava-colored evening (somewhere a tree tuft passes through the moon's ring). (Elsewhere, at the most shining hour, four cupidons holding a stick of sugar cane and prancing on small golden wheels cause a blue and white milk like seawater to rise into the over-verdant field.) And now, in the blue, a young Bacchic face appears, red with anger and superhuman gaiety, his eyes sparkling and cynical, his lips twisted with gibes and insults! But the dull blows of a knife chopping meat tell me clearly enough where I am, as do a woman's two arms, red to the elbows with blood like tobacco juice, which extract packets of entrails from the depths of a great mother-of-pearl carcass. An iron basin flashes when overturned. In the autumn light pink and gold, I see the entire bank of this canal hidden from my view by pulleys drawing blocks of ice, baskets of pigs, heavy bunches of bananas, streaming clusters of oysters, and barrels of edible fish as big as sharks and as shining as porcelain. I still have the strength to note the scales at the time when a foot placed on the platform and a fist clamped on the bronze chain are about to tip the monstrous heap of watermelons, pumpkins, and bundles of sugarcane tied with creepers that sprout bursts of flowers colored like mouths. And suddenly, raising my head, I find myself seated on a stair of the landing, with my hand in my cat's fur.

[March 1899]

Concerning the Brain

The brain is an organ. The student will acquire a solid principle if he firmly grasps that the nervous system is homogeneous in its center and ramifications, and that its function is simply such as its mechanical efficiency determines. Nothing justifies the excessive belief that ascribes to white or grey matter not only a sensitive or motor activity, but also the function of "secreting" intelligence and will, as noise secretes a semblance of words, and the liver bile. The brain is an organ, like the digestive and circulatory systems; the nervous system has its precise function, which is the production of sensation and movement.

I use the word "production" purposely. It would be inexact to see the nerves as simple threads, agents inert in themselves of a dual transmission, on one hand "afferent" (as it is said), on the other "efferent," ready ad libitum to telegraph a noise, a shock, or an order of the inner mind. The apparatus ensures the opening and expansion of the cerebral wave, as constant as a pulse. Sensation is not a passive phenomenon; it is a special state of activity. I compare it to a vibrating chord on which the noise is focused by the correct position of the finger. By sensation I ascertain facts; by movement I control action. But the vibration is constant.

And this view allows us to further our investigation. All vibration implies a source, as every circle a center. The source of nervous vibration resides in the brain, which, separate from all other organs, fills the entire cavity of the closed skull.

The rule of analogy indicated at the outset prevents us from seeing there anything but the agent of reception, transformation, and, as it were, digestion of the initial disturbance. One may imagine that this function devolves especially to the peripheral matter; that the white substratum constitutes a manner of amplification and composition; and, finally, that the complex organs at the base of the brain are so many workshops of practical application: switchboard, keyboard, and meters, the apparatuses of connection and adjustment.

We must now consider vibration itself. By this I mean a movement, both dual and unitary, by which a body proceeds from one point to return to it. It is the very "element," the radical symbol that is the essential constituent of all life. The vibration of our brain is the bubbling of life's wellspring, the emotion of matter in contact with divine unity, whose ascendancy constitutes our very personality. It is the umbilical cord of our dependency. Our nerves, and the contact they give us with the external world, are only tools of our knowledge, and in this sense alone are they the conditions of it. As one learns to use a tool, so do we educate our senses. We learn to know the world by its contact with our intimate identity.

The brain is, then, nothing but an organ: the organ of animal knowledge, merely sensitive in beasts, intelligible in man. Yet if it is only a particular organ, it cannot be the support of intelligence, or soul. One cannot do this wrong to part of our body, which is the active living image of every God. The human soul is that by which the human body is what it is, its act, its continuously operant seed, and, as the Schoolmen tell us, its *form*.

[1899]

Leaving the Land

It is the sea that has come to get us. It pulls at our moorings, draws us from the gangway. With a great shudder the ship little by little increases the distances that separate it from the congested wharf and the human scale of things. And we follow the lazy windings of the quiet slow-moving river. This is one of the mouths where the earth overflows and, bursting in a doughy mass, comes to chew the sea mixed with its herbage. Of the land where we lived, nothing remains but the color, the green soul ready to liquefy. And already before us, in the limpid air, a lighthouse shows the dividing line and the marine desert.

While we are eating, I feel we have stopped, and sense the respiration of the open sea in the entire body of the ship and in my own. The pilot is going ashore. In the electric lamplight of his small dancing boat, he salutes our liberated ship. The ladder is cast off and we leave. We leave by the light of the moon!

And I see above me the curved line of the horizon like the bounds of a measureless sleep. Desperately my whole heart flees the receding shore behind us, like the heavy sob we utter in the night when we return to sleep. Ah, sea! it is you! I am coming home. There is no breast as good as eternity, no safety like space unlimited. Henceforth the news of the world will be that which is brought to us each evening by the moon's face as it rises on our left. I am delivered from diversity and change: no vicissitudes but those of night and day, no projects but the sky we see, no resting place but the bosom of the great waters mirroring the sky. Cleansing purity! Here with me, to absolve us, is the Absolute! What do I care now for the ferments of peoples, the intrigues of marriages and wars, the transactions of gold and economic forces, the whole confused game played back there? Everything is reduced to facts and the multiple passions of men and things. Whereas I possess the central rhythm in its essence, the alternation of day and night, and the simple fact of the starry bodies that appear on the horizon at the appointed hour. And all day long I study the sea as you read the eyes of a woman who understands, as you read her thought with the attention of one who listens. Of what worth to me are the gross deformations of your tragedies and pageants compared to this pure mirror?

[October 1899]

1900–1905

The Lamp and the Bell

One is the sign, the other the expression of the expectancy of the universe (and of my misfortune to be alive); one is time itself, the other a suddenly echoing moment. One measures the silence, the other deepens the darkness; one entreats, the other fascinates me. Oh suspense! Oh bitter patience! Dual watchfulness, the one on flame, the other calculating!

Night takes away our proof, we no longer know where we are. Lines and colors, our passionate arrangement of the world about us (whose center we carry with us wherever we go according to the angles from which at any moment our gaze makes its report), are no longer there to confirm our position. We are reduced to ourselves alone. Our vision no longer has the visible for limit, but the invisible for place of solitary confinement—homogeneous, immediate, indifferent, compact. In the heart of this darkness the lamp is somewhere, some thing. It appears wholly alive! It contains its oil; by virtue of its flame, it drinks itself. It bears witness to that of which the entire abyss is the absence. As it has drawn profit from the previous evening, it will endure until the sky's pink fire, and the hazy vapors like a new wine's froth! Its store of gold will last until dawn. As for me, let me not perish in the night! Let me die in light alone!

But if night shuts our eyes, it is that we may listen all the more, not only with our ears, but with all the audition of our souls breathing in the manner of fish. Something in the vast void gathers, ripens a number that is fired like a gun. I hear the bell like the need to speak, like the resolution of our visceral silence, the very word within the word. During the day, with stubborn force or in short bursts, we keep hearing the sentence woven on a continuous stave by all beings bonded by the duty of the chorus. Night puts an end to it, and only *measure* remains. (I am alive, I lend my ear.) Of what whole is it a part? What *movement* does it beat? What *time*? Here, to show it, is the artifice of hourglass and waterclock; the clock's trap forces the hour to explode. As for me, I am alive. I am brought back once more into a relationship with time; I am *regulated* in accordance with such and such a progression and particular number of hours. I have my escapement, I contain the creative pulse. Outside of me the stroke that suddenly reverberates attests to all the hidden labor of my heart, the motor and worker of my body.

Just as the navigator hugging the shore notes all the lighthouses one by one, so the astronomer, halfway between the horizons, standing on the moving earth like a sailor on his bridge, calculates the total hour with his eyes on the most complete clockface of all. The plot of the huge sign! The numberless universe reduced to establishing its own proportions, elaborating its own distances! No period of stellar motion is devised without our assent, no plan is drawn by the world concert without our involvement, no star is revealed by the microscope on the photographic plate without my self being the negative. The hour strikes by the agency of the huge lighted sky! From the clock in the depths of a sickroom to the great flaming Angel who reaches in turn all points of the sky prescribed for its circular flight, there is an exact response. I do not serve to calculate any hour but this. I mark it with a resolve no less firm.

[1902]

The Deliverance of Amaterasu

No mortal could seriously honor the Moon with public devotion. She is the accountant and fabricator of our months, the spinner of a thread sparingly measured. In the good clear light of day we rejoice to see all things together, beautiful like an ample, many-colored cloth; but as soon as evening comes or when night has already fallen, I find once again the fatal Shuttle deeply engaged in its passage across the celestial weft. My lady friend, let your eye, lit with a mischievous light, confess that it is so, and those five fingernails that shine on the neck of your lute.

Yet does the sun, ever pure and youthful, ever like itself, most radiant and most white, lack anything each day for its glory to blossom, its countenance to smile? And who shall look at it without immediately feeling obliged to laugh? Let us give our hearts to the good sun with laughter as free as when we greet a lovely child. Can it be that it finds a mirror for its red face in the narrowest rut at the bend of a public thoroughfare, and that only man's secret soul stays so closed that it does not reflect its likeness, and a little gold in the depths of its shadows?

Scarcely had the grumpy race of Sons of the Soil begun to splash about on the breast of the nourishing earth than they forgot, in their mad haste to eat, the shining evidence, the eternal Epiphany in which they had been allowed to live. As the diligent engraver who applies himself to cutting his plank along the grain pays scant attention to the lamp over his head that supplies him with light, so the farmer reduced all things to his own two hands and his buffalo's dark rump, forgetful of the universe's luminous heart and caring only to dig his furrow straight. Then Amaterasu grew indignant in the sunlight. She is the sun's soul by which it shines, like the breath of a sounding trumpet. "When the beast has satisfied its belly, it loves me," she said; "it enjoys my caress in all simplicity; it sleeps in the warmth of my face, full of the regular beat of its blood on the surface of its body, the inner pulse of red life. But brute impious man has never enough to eat. The flower worships me all day long and feeds its devout heart on the virtue of my face. Man alone on his stem is ill at heart; he hides from me the sacred mirror within himself that is made for my reflection. Let us therefore flee. Let us hide our unhonored beauty!" Straightaway, like a dove that slips into a hole in the wall, she went into a deep cavern at the mouth of the Yokigawa River and hermetically sealed the opening with a huge boulder.

Suddenly, it grew dark and, at one stroke, the sky as it is by day appeared with all its stars. It was not night but the very darkness that there was before the world, positive shadow. Raw and terrible night touched the living earth. There was great absence in the sky: space had lost its center; the sun's person had left like one who goes away to avoid seeing you, or a judge who quits his court. Then these ingrates knew the beauty of Amaterasu. Let them look for her now in the lifeless air! A great groan spread through the islands, the agony that is penitence, the abomination that is fear. As myriads of mosquitoes fill the noxious evening air, the earth was given over to the brigandage of the demons and the dead, distinguished from the quick by their having no navel. As the pilot of a ship puts out his near lights to see more clearly in the dark, they saw a strange otherworldly whiteness like the frontier of a neighboring world, or the reflection of a future sun.

Then all the gods and goddesses, the unofficial and domestic spirits that help man and are his close companions in the manner of horses and oxen, were moved by the furless creature's miserable cries, like the yelping of little dogs. And at the mouth of the Yokigawa River all of them, those of the sea and air such as herds of buffaloes, schools of sardines, flights of starlings, gathered together at the mouth of the Yokigawa torrent where the virgin Amaterasu hid in a hole in the earth like honeycomb in the hollow of a tree, or treasure in a jar.

"A lamp is darkened only by a light still brighter. Amaterasu is there," they said. "We do not see her, yet we know she has not left us. Her glory has not suffered loss. She has hidden in the earth like a cicada, or an ascete within his own thought. How will we make her come out? What bait shall we use? What can we offer her that will be as beautiful as she?"

Immediately they made a very pure, perfectly round mirror from a stone that had fallen from the sky. They tore down a pine tree and swathed it like a doll in gold and scarlet raiments. They decked it like a woman and gave it the mirror for its face. And they put the sacred *gohei* upright opposite the cavern that was full of the pouch that contained the indignant soul of light.

What voice, powerful enough to pierce the earth, did they choose to say, "Amaterasu, I am here? I am here and we know you are there too. Be present, vision of my eyes! Come out from the grave, Oh life!" The familiar voice, the first voice she hears as she crosses the threshold of humankind, the cock crowing at the first red streak of dawn everywhere on the farms! He is the clarion call, the trumpet that no darkness can quiet. Night and day, indifferent to the visible presence or remoteness of his god, he tirelessly blows his fanfare, he gives precise utterance of the faith. So, before Amaterasu in the earth, they brought the great white bird. And he crowed straightaway. And having crowed, he crowed again.

All the noises of life immediately stirred as if they could not fail to respond to his summons—the murmur of day—the active, endless grammatical statement, the continuous progression of milling words punctuated by the bonze with his wooden mallet in the depths of the temple; all the gods, scarcely distinct from the names that contain them, were heard at one time. The sound was very timid, very low. But in the earth Amaterasu heard them and was surprised.

And here one should glue the image of Uzume, in the very way she breaks into the dark shower of printed characters in small popular books. The good goddess had invented everything! She it was who devised the grand scheme. Here she was boldly dancing on the tight skin of her drum, as frenzied as hope itself! And all she found to do to free the sun was to sing a poor song like those that little children make up: *Hito futa miyo* . . .

Hito futa miyo
Itsa muyu nana
Yokokono tari
Momochi yoroduzu

which means, One, two, three, four, five, six, seven, eight, nine, ten, a hundred, a thousand, ten thousand; and which also means, All of you, look at the door—Her Majesty appears, hurrah!—Our hearts are satisfied.—Look at my belly and my thighs.

For in the fury of the dance she untied her belt and impatiently cast it aside, and with an open robe, laughing and crying, stamped her feet and jumped on the resonant elastic skin she labored with her strong heels. And when they saw her body full and vigorous like that of a small girl, comfort came to their hearts and they began to laugh. The sun was no longer in the sky yet there were no laments. They were laughing! Amaterasu heard them and her heart was mortified. Unable to overcome her curiosity, she softly set the door ajar: "Why are you laughing?"

A great dazzling ray of light swept over the assembled gods, crossed the edge of the earth, lit the moon in the empty sky. Suddenly the day star blazed in the lifeless sky. As an oversize fruit bursts, or as a mother opens herself to the child who forces its way with its head, look! the blind earth could no longer contain the jealous Eye, the burning curiosity of Fire placed in its center, the woman who is the Sun! "Why do you laugh?" "O Amaterasu," said Uzume.

(And at the same time all the gods said, "O Amaterasu!" and these words ended their prayer.)

"Oh Amaterasu, you were not with us, did you think you had left us without your face? But look, here is she who is fairer than you. Look!" she said, showing the *gohei,* the sacred mirror that concentrated the flame and created an unbearable brilliance. "Look!"

She looked; and jealous, rapturous, astonished, fascinated, she took one step outside the cavern; and instantly night was no more. All the great worlds that turn around the sun like an eagle about his prey were surprised to see the day burst forth in an unaccustomed place, and the little earth consumed in glory like a candlestick in its own light.

She took one step outside the cavern and straightaway the strongest of all the gods leapt forward to close the door behind her. And there, upright before her own image surrounded by the seven rainbows— spirit adorable, living fire, of which only two pink hands and two pink feet and the curls of her hair together with her divine face could be seen—she, the young, the formidable!—the essential, the explosive soul! And as the lark rises in ever wider circles above its sparkling goal, Amaterasu, reconquered by her image, climbed up once again toward the celestial throne. And there was a new time, the first day.

—At the gate of Shinto temples, by means of a rope made of straw, the Earth still forbids the Sun to enter its depths like the wife who showed her breasts to her rebel husband. And in the last recess of the bare sanctuary, instead of the Eleusinian fire, a small round mirror of polished metal lies hidden.

[1902]

Visit

Many shouts are needed, and furious beating on the long-suffering door, before the servant inside at last grows aware of the concert and comes to acknowledge the stranger who has been deposited in a wooden case at the door. For here no echoing bell, no alarm attached by a wire through the walls to the most secret parts, suddenly determines an explosion like the yelp of a dog you pinch. The Black Mountain is the district of the well-established families, and its silence is deep. The space that Europeans use for recreation and games, the Chinese give over to retreat. In the midst of the animal concoction, between streets bubbling with an impure humanity, they set aside places for leisure, protected by wide empty enclosures or property inherited from some kithless person together with ancient household gods. Let a noble roof alone accommodate the huge shade of these banyans older than the city, these lichis tottering under the weight of their purple acorns! I have gone inside; I wait; I am alone in the parlor; it is four o'clock. The rain has stopped, or is it still falling? The earth has received its fill of water: the drenched leaves breathe at their ease. As for me, under this dark kindly sky, I taste the compunction and peace you feel when you have shed tears. Facing me there is an uneven-topped wall in which three square windows, barred by porcelain bamboos, are open. As you adjust a grill on diplomatic papers to isolate the words that matter, so this screen, with its triple opening, has been applied to a landscape of overabundant leafage and water, and has reduced it to the theme and responses of a triptych. The frame makes the picture; the bars that allow my glance to pass exclude and confine me here better than a bolted door. My host does not come, I am alone.

[1902]

Rice

By the iron blade we sink our teeth into the very earth, and already our bread eats there in the way we shall eat it. The sun, in our cold northern lands, must knead the dough. It ripens our fields just as the naked flame cooks our cakes and roasts our meat. With a strong ploughshare we open a furrow in the solid earth where the crust is formed that we cut with our knives and grind with our jaws.

But here, in the East, the sun does not only serve to heat the domestic sky like an oven full of coals. One must ruse with it. As soon as the year begins the waters flow—menses of the virgin soil. These vast fields without slopes, barely divided from the sea that they prolong and that the rain soaks without flowing away, take refuge as soon as they conceive beneath the enduring sheet of water fixed in place by a thousand frames. And the work of the village consists of enriching the sauce with many tubs of water: on all fours the farmer, in the midst, stirs and mixes it with his hands. The yellow man does not bite his bread; he snatches it with his lips and swallows the semi-liquid food without molding it in his mouth. Thus the rice grows, as it is cooked, in steam. And the people's whole care is to give it the water it needs, and to tend the even heat of the heavenly furnace. So, when the waters rise, the lines of peasants sing like cicadas. And the buffalo is not needed. Side by side, the man and woman clutch the same bar and press the red blade as one, with the same knee, as it were; they tend the kitchen of their field as a housewife her steaming meal. And the Annamite draws water in a kind of spoon; as yellow as mustard, with his black cassock and little tortoise head, he is the sad sexton of the mire. How many reverences and genuflections there are when the peasant couple, with a bucket tied to two ropes, go looking in every nook for the slushy juice to anoint the earth that is good to eat!

[1903]

The Full Stop

I come to a halt. My walk is marked by a stop like a sentence you write: it is the inscription on a grave here at my feet, at this bend where the road goes down. From here I have my last view of the earth; I consider the land of the dead, which spreads out wide, with its bouquets of pines and olive trees, amid the deep harvests that edge it. All is consummated in fullness: Ceres has embraced Proserpine. All things resist exodus, trace a limit. I find again the great vertical line of the river at the foot of the unchanging mountains; I recognize our boundary, and acquiesce. My absence is figured by this island thronged with the dead and consumed by harvests. Standing alone amongst a buried people, with my feet between the names spoken by the grass, I watch for the opening in the earth to which for the last two days the gentle breeze, like a dog that has lost its bark, has been pushing the huge cloud brought from out of the Waters behind me. All is over: the day has come to an end. I can do nothing but turn around and once more take the measure of the path that binds me to my home. Here, where the porters of coffins and funeral tubs make a halt, I look for a long while at the yellow road that leads from the living to the dead and whose endpoint is a red dot in the overcast sky, like a smoldering fire.

[1903]

Libation to the Coming Day

I have climbed to the mountain top to toast the future day (the new day, the one that is to come, perhaps it follows this very night); to the topmost peak of the mountain that lifts a goblet of ice to Aurora's lips! I am naked in it; it was so full as I entered, it overflowed like a cataract. I dance in the bubbling source like a grape seed in a glass of champagne. I cannot distinguish the gushing couch that I press with my belly and knees from the gulf of air separated from me by a thin edge. Beneath me the shrill eagle soars. Fair Aurora! You come here in a single bound from the sea below among the islands! Drink, so that to the very soles of my feet, deep in this liquor where I bathe, I feel your quivering lip. Let the sun rise, so that I may see the weightless shadow of my suspended body painted beneath me on the sands of this swimming-pool, surrounded by the seven-hued rainbow!

[1903]

The Day of the Feast-of-All-Rivers

On the day of the Feast-of-All-Rivers we have gone to celebrate our very own, which is wide and swift. It is the country's outlet, the force enclosed within its flanks, the liquefaction of the earth's substance, the explosion of liquid water hidden in its most secret folds and of the milk drawn by the Ocean that suckles it. Here, beneath the good old granite bridge, between the boats that come down from the mountains bringing us ore and sugar, and, on the other side, the junks of the many-colored sea caught in the fishhooks of their anchors and turning their great patient eyes like beasts of burden toward the untraversable piles, the river issues forth by sixty arches. What an uproar, what a snowy whiteness it makes when Dawn blows its trumpet, or when Evening departs to the beat of a drum! It has no embankment like the cheerless sewers of the West; on a level with its flow, in domestic familiarity, everybody comes to wash their clothes and draw water for supper. Even in spring, in turbulent playfulness, the dragon invades our streets and houses in bubbling coils. As the Chinese mother presents her small child to the household dog so that it can carefully clean its backside, so does the river wipe the city's huge filth with a lick of its tongue.

But today is its feast. In its company we celebrate its carnival in the roiling tumult of the flaxen waters. If you cannot spend the day deep in the eddies in the shade of your boat like a buffalo up to its eyes, do not forget to offer the midday sun a bowl of pure water in a white porcelain bowl; it will be a remedy for colic in the coming year. And it is no time to be stingy: let the heavy jug be unsealed, the golden drinking gourd with its earthenware crust from which you suck the tea of the fourth month by the very neck! Let each one, on this afternoon of flood-tide and full sunshine, come to feel, and strike, and embrace, and ride the great municipal river, the water-animal that flees to the sea on its endless spine. Everything from one bank to another is swarming and trembling with sampans and boats where the silken guests, like bright bouquets, drink and play; all is splendor and noise of drums. From here and there, on all sides, appear pirogues with dragons' heads that quickly glide along, driven by the arms of a hundred naked paddlers roused to a delirious pitch by a tall yellow man who beats a demonic rhythm! So slender are they, they seem a furrow, the very arrow of the current churned by the entire row of bodies plunging in the waters up to their waists. On the bank where I embark a woman is washing her linen; the deep-red lacquer bowl in which she heaps her ragged clothes has a golden edge that shines and blazes in the sun of this solemn celebration. The brute glance of a created lightning flash; eye of the honorable river's feast.

[1903]

The Yellow Hour

This is the most golden hour of the entire year! As the farmer at the end of the season reaps the fruits of his toil and gathers his reward, so there comes the golden hour to transmute all things in heaven and earth. I walk in the interval of the harvest up to my neck in gold; I put my chin on the table lit by the sun at the furthest limit of the field; I go up to the hills and survey the sea of grain. Between the banks of grass and the huge dry flame of the day-colored plain, where is the old dark earth? The water is changed to wine; oranges glow in the silent branches. All is ripe—grain and straw, and the fruit with the leaf. It is indeed golden; all has come to an end and I see that all is true. In the fervent labor of the year that vaporizes every color, suddenly to my eyes the earth is like a sun! Let me not perish before the most golden hour.

[1905]

Dissolution

And once more I am carried back over the indifferent liquid sea. When I am dead, no one will ever hurt me again. When I am buried between my father and mother, no one will ever hurt me again. No one will ever laugh again at this heart that loves too much. In the belly of the earth the sacrament of my body will be dissolved, but my heart, like the most piercing cry, will rest in Abraham's bosom. Now all is dissolved, and I vainly seek with heavy eye the familiar landscape, and the solid road beneath my feet, and that cruel face. The sky is nothing but mist, space nothing but water. As you see, all is dissolved, and I would look in vain about me for line or form. There is no horizon but the cessation of the deepest color. All matter is brought together into water alone, like the tears I feel flowing down my cheeks; and all sound is like the respiration of sleep when our breath comes from regions within that are deafest to hope. I look in vain, I no longer find anything outside me, either the land that was my home, or that much loved face.

[1905]

Notes on the Poems

The Coconut Palm

First publication: *La Nouvelle Revue*, 15 September 1895

Claudel wrote this first poem after a nine-day visit to Colombo on the outward-bound journey to China, his boat having been delayed for repairs. He explored the city and nearby region. "The tropical countries I saw in passing have a charm for me that I cannot forget," he told Mallarmé in a letter sent shortly after his arrival in Shanghai.

Pagoda

First publication: *La Revue de Paris*, 15 August 1896

Eleven months separate the publication of "The Coconut Palm" from that of "Pagoda." During the interval Claudel had settled in China. "Pagoda" commemorated his visit to the monastery of Long-Houa in Shanghai, though, as the last line notes, he "did not know its name." *Moxas* are cauterized flesh wounds that here signify religious commitment.

The City at Night

First publication: *La Revue de Paris*, 15 August 1896

Shanghai is "dense, naïve, and disordered" but not foreign, as it were, for it calls up the familiar life of the great cities of the past. The art of the Claudel prose poem as an internally resonant, multilayered composition is already fully achieved. As he later wrote, echoing Ecclesiasticus 32:3, "My poetic doctrine may be summed up in the words of ancient Wisdom: *Do not hinder music. Let it emanate of its own accord. Make sure it emanates.*"

Gardens

First publication: *La Revue de Paris*, 15 August 1896

The opening line, evocative of the Shanghai morning mist, reminds us that white is the color of mourning in China. *Foumao* refers to the coarse long-hooded headgear worn by Chinese peasants. The poetic force of the conclusion is emphasized in the original manuscript by a lyrical development in which the poet wakes in the night, sees Orion and the autumn star hanging like "the radiant face of Joy's madness," and thinks, "Over there is a garden, the sleeping waters reflect a golden star." He opted for an elliptic close.

The Feast of the Dead in the Seventh Month

First publication: *La Revue blanche*, 1 July 1897

"La Fête des morts du septième mois" treats the ritual ceremonies for the dead that Claudel attended early in his stay in Shanghai, at a time when he was writing his play *Le Repos du Septième Jour*. The sombre note of the *dies tremenda*, the "fearful day," recurs at intervals in the collection.

Sea Thoughts

First publication: *Connaissance de l'Est*, 1900

The sea journey between Shanghai and Foochow (today's Fuzhou), where Claudel took up the temporary charge of vice-consul in March 1896, frames the remembered images of his return to France from the United States the previous year. Leaving Boston in February, he stopped over in Paris, then went to his family home in the Champagne village of Villeneuve-sur-Fère. A group of poems in rhyming alexandrines on the theme of exile, composed at the same time as many of the poems in *Knowing the East* but not published as a series until 1950, bears the title *Vers d'exil*: "Paul, il nous faut partir pour un départ plus beau . . . ," ("Paul, we must leave for a finer place . . ."); again: "Cheval, on t'a en vain mis le mors dans la bouche . . ." ("Horse, they vainly put the bit in your mouth . . .").

Cities

First publication: *La Revue blanche*, 1 July 1897

"There is a study to be made of cities and of the way an organ is little by little differentiated in the midst of floating mankind," Claudel wrote. Cities are a constant theme in his work: one thinks of his play, *La Ville* of 1893, and of his later *Conversations dans le Loir-et-Cher*. He was a shade less critical of Boston when he first moved there in 1893: "Boston is entirely red, but of a lighter and healthier red than Manhattan's formidable chocolate. All the housefronts bulge out into the streets, and the effect is unpleasant. I live in the topmost district of this astonishing city . . ."

Theater

First publication: *La Revue blanche*, 1 July 1897

The piece commemorates a visit to Canton (today's Guangzhou) in March 1896, the corporation mentioned in the opening being one of the many trade guilds that flourished in the Chinese ports and enjoyed considerable power. In Canton the local corporation, especially strong, owned its own theater. Claudel was taken by the Chinese theater even before he left for the East, since he and his sister Camille had enthusiastically acclaimed the performances they attended in Paris. He later used some traditional Chinese techniques in his plays.

Graves — Noises

First publication: *La Revue blanche*, 1 July 1897

The double-barreled title does not so much refer to a loosely fitting pair of images as to the resonance of each with each, like life-in-death. Claudel writes the first of his Foochow texts, which comprise some of his finest poems. Much attention will be paid to the auditory imagination throughout *Knowing the East*, notably in "The Bell."

The Entrance to the Earth

First publication: *La Revue blanche*, 1 July 1897

After his bleak stay in Shanghai, Claudel found Foochow to be a paradise. He went for long walks in and around the treaty port and capital of Fukien province, a center of the tea trade. The region is mountainous, the climate subtropical, the forests rich in fir, pine, and rosewood. He goes alone and ecstatic.

Religion of the Sign

First publication: *La Revue blanche*, 1 July 1897

Claudel had found in Mallarmé a man of letters who treated the form, sound, and meaning of words as devoutly as ritual. He himself was drawn to meditate on the significance of ideograms, not only Chinese but those he discerned with not a little humor in Western languages (thus English *tree:* "the tall tree in the foreground, the stream at its base, the double "e" representing graceful meanders as in the Christmas cards of Mr. Tuck"; and *it*: "a man who looks at a signpost"). He commented, "Is it absurd to think that the alphabet is the abridgement and vestige of all the acts, gestures, attitudes and, consequently, feelings of man at the heart of the creation surrounding him?"

The Banyan

First publication: *La Revue blanche*, 1 July 1897

The place of the tree is large in Claudel's imagination as shown in this volume already in "The Coconut Tree," but also later "The Pine-Tree," "The Golden Ark in the Forest," and elsewhere. Though he had first encountered the "sublime" banyan in Colombo, Foochow was the ideal place to continue his study since it was known as the City of Banyans—trees not, however, of the same species as the *ficus benghalensis*.

Toward the Mountain

First publication: *Connaissance de l'Est*, 1900

In line with the exuberance of the Foochow texts, "Vers la montagne" refers to a brief stay in the mountain resort of Kuliang in the summer of 1896. Claudel, like Rimbaud, is one of the great walker poets who venture forth in the morning, "when a man and his memories have not woken at the same time." It is then, he observes, that "a kind of open hypnosis arises, a very curious state of pure receptivity."

The Upper Sea

First publication: *Connaissance de 1'Est*, 1900

The enthusiasm of the previous text is transmuted in these lines, which again allude to his excursion of June 1896 in the mountains of Kuliang, by means of a visionary evocation. Dream images have a significant place in the collection.

The Temple of Consciousness

First publication: *Connaissance de l'Est*, 1900

Claudel visited the monastery of Kuchian four times in the Spring, Summer and Autumn of 1896, and spoke of it as the "temple of consciousness," surrounded by the enormous star of the countryside. It stood on a high peak; and deep below, still more remote and accessible only by a stairway, was a cave inhabited by a lone hermit.

October

First publication: *Connaissance de l'Est*, 1900

In October 1926, thirty years after writing "October," Claudel noted that this poem would be "a thing to read at my graveside." The refrain echoes the words of John 19:30: "Consummatum est"—"It is finished"—after the Crucifixion.

November

First publication: *Connaissance de l'Est*, 1900

Claudel's love for rural life and virginal nature is given expression, from the naïve to the oneiric. The foxes mentioned in the second last paragraph recall perhaps the errant spirits of Chinese legend; here more truly, they are phantasms of the poet himself like those of his adolescent play *L'Endormie*.

Painting

First publication: *Connaissance de l'Est*, 1900

As the future author of many texts on the visual arts, especially *L'Oeil écoute*, Claudel was much attracted to Chinese and Japanese painting. He "paints" his poem, like the Chinese painter "of fine and limpid heart" whom Mallarmé depicted in an early piece, but the scene is not static: each object and figure move to the presiding rhythm.

The Contemplative

First publication: *Connaissance de l'Est*, 1900

In December 1896 Claudel visited the Buddhist Monastery of Yong-fu built in the cave of a mountain near Foochow. He imagines himself a hermit who will be fed, like the prophet Eli, by some crow. The image of the crow occurs frequently in Claudel, who was to be told that his name could be rendered in Japanese as "Black Bird in the Rising Sun," a title later given to a collection of his essays on Japan.

December

First publication: *Connaissance de l'Est*, 1900

The poem marks the "pause" and "suspension" that separates the nine-month period Claudel spent in his beloved Foochow before returning to Shanghai, where he had much less agreeable consular duties. The Fukien landscape is felt with the hand, tasted with the mind.

Storm

First publication: *Connaissance de l'Est*, 1900

Claudel left Foochow for Shanghai in December 1896, on a sea frequently subject to violent storms. On this occasion the ship advances valiantly; but the following year, on his return voyage from Shanghai to Foochow, he would feel his last day had come, and "Peril of the Sea" translates an "intrusion into the uninhabitable."

The Pig

First publication: *Connaissance de l'Est*, 1900

Claudel claimed "rural" qualities wholly opposed to Parisian refinement. As vice-consul in Foochow, he often had to deal with questions concerning pigs, for Spanish missionaries would complain to him that converts were being robbed of their animals, thereby growing estranged to the Church. In writing this poem, Claudel was doubtless influenced by the Jules Renard of "Histoires naturelles," though the phonetic, rhythmic, and metaphoric zest is all the more robustly his own; and to this must be added the savory philosophical salt, no less droll, that Claudel finds in his theme.

Drifting

First publication: *La Revue blanche*, 15 August 1897

The original title, as the manuscript shows, was "Le Fleuve," that is, the Yang-tse. In March 1897 Claudel was appointed to Hankow ("an infernal place"), where for six months he was in charge of the vice-consulate. His main task was to negotiate French participation in building the Hankow-Peking railway (the contract was successfully obtained, and signed in June). Hankow stands on the left bank of the Han River, where it joins the Yang-tse some 600 miles from the coast. Claudel here plunges into its flooding waters. As he later told a young poet, "The only way to be a true source is to swallow and digest the ocean."

Doors

First publication: *La Revue blanche*, 15 August 1897

The pretext may well have been Claudel's visit to the vice-roy in the administrative city of Wuchang in April 1897 during negotiations for the Hankow-Peking railway. From the first enigmatic words the poem moves in an atmosphere of strangeness where opposites paradoxically meet, at once opening and closure, door and wall, setting sun and rising moon, princess and old man, life and death.

The River

First publication: *La Revue blanche*, 15 August 1897

The poem is once more the occasion for Claudel to evoke the primal force of water, here again the Yang-tse. It was a time of drought in the land, and he saw great quantities of calves' hides being brought down by the river. "The Chinese peasant," he wrote, "despite his superstitions, is clearly obliged to sacrifice these animals to feed on their meat." But the Yang-tse is life itself—more, spiritual renewal.

Rain

First publication: *La Revue blanche*, 15 September 1898

The pouring rain of Hankow resembles a prison, both protective and comforting, and the poem in parallel fashion is a happily enclosed drop of ink.

Night on the Verandah

First publication: *La Revue blanche*, 15 September 1898

The poet here uses a manner of simultaneous technique at far remove from any narration. Legend, astronomy, ritual, the art of photography metaphorize a hymn to the night.

The Moon's Splendor

First publication: *La Revue blanche*, 15 September 1898

Claudel writes another of the poems that date from the summer of 1897, no doubt after the successful completion of his Hankow negotiations. It is a companion piece to "Night on the Verandah," but introduces in the last lines the image of the small discreet star of heart's desire that will recur in the poet's later writing.

Dreams

First publication: *La Revue blanche*, 15 September 1898

Claudel amplifies the serial technique used in "Night on the Verandah," the seven parts of his poem conveying diverse states of semi-consciousness from magical vision to remembered childhood. Thus the fifth paragraph presents the oneiric disarrangement, akin to that of several Rimbaud poems, of east, south, and west, of island and sky, of African, Italian, and Cycladic.

Heat

First publication: *Connaissance de l'Est*, 1900

The happy mood of the three preceding poems is broken by "Heat," which captures the harshness of the Hankow summer. Nothing can escape the sun's force, like a purifying flame.

Considering the City

First publication: *Connaissance de l'Est*, 1900

It was in the high altitudes of the Kuliang mountains that Claudel saw clouds forming the "city of the triple mountain." He composes a vision of the divine city in a moment of "huge suspense," and his densely layered style and, in particular, his technique of multiple negation possess a prophetic strangeness.

Going down the River

First publication: *Connaissance de l'Est*, 1900

Never before in the prose poems had Claudel expressed such a degree of enthusiasm as in this poem, a Rimbaldian "illumination," which celebrates the joy of color as he goes down the Yang-tse.

The Bell

First publication: *Connaissance de l'Est*, 1900

Claudel took much interest in popular legend, both Western and Oriental. He refashions here a story by the writer, translator, and teacher Lafcadio Hearn (1850–1904), taken from the collection *Some Chinese Ghosts*; but he had perhaps also consulted the book that Hearn himself used, *La Piété filiale en Chine*, published in 1877. A French consul who had lived for many years in China, P. Dabry de Thiersant translated twenty-five stories from the work *Pe-Hiaou-Tou-Chou* ("A Hundred Examples of Filial Piety"), piety being, as the scholar-translator observed, "the single pivot of the whole machine that drives the huge mass of people." The last story becomes in Hearn poignantly "The Soul of the Great Bell," and in Claudel, via Hearn, but with visionary and auditory resonance, "The Bell." K'ang-hsi, the second and greatest Manchu emperor, from 1661 to 1722, was an exceptional patron of learning and the arts.

The Tomb

First publication: *Connaissance de l'Est*, 1900

The second of the Nanking texts strikes a bitter note: Claudel records his visit to the necropolis of the Ming dynasty and, in particular, the tomb of the first emperor. The mighty have fallen, the bricks have been torn away, the peasants have built their homes with the imperial ruins. Not here the exultant poet, he had recently completed his play, *Le Repos du septième jour*, which he described as an enquiry into the essence of death. He had been much affected by death as he witnessed it at close quarters in his family, and feared above all the thought of a destiny deprived of salvation. As he noted in the margins of his Chinese play, "O my God! Hell is much more awful than I have written here, and who can imagine its horror! One mortal sin can condemn me to it." This was the background to his faith. As he later said of *Knowing the East,* "A threat hangs over the book like the extreme lucidity of days before typhoons."

Claudel uses the erudite word *xénodoques,* which originally meant a place for greeting and lodging the foreign guests of noble Greeks; it aptly serves the Chinese context.

The Sadness of Water

First publication: *Connaissance de l'Est,* 1900

The poem commemorates a visit in January 1898 to the Chusan archipelago, a "region of sadness," seen in the rain. But more than to local color, Claudel is sensitive to the deep mixture of joy and bitterness inherent in the creative act. He is the peasant of the last lines; perhaps also the goose.

Sailing by Night

First publication: *Connaissance de l'Est,* 1900

Claudel wrote this page after a voyage in a houseboat on the Yang-tse in January 1898. The mood of confident patience is sustained by the image in the last lines of a lone star, which mirrors that of "The Moon's Splendor" like a similarly gracious sign.

Halt on the Canal

First publication: *Connaissance de l'Est,* 1900

From the initial "Yet . . ." which marks a symbolic boundary, the poem expands in a circular manner around an empty centre like the saying quoted from the Tao-te-ching, "the Way." Form and meaning correspond.

The Pine Tree

First publication: *Connaissance de l'Est*, 1900

In a still more detailed manner than in the earlier pages devoted to the co-
conut palm and the banyan, Claudel "explicates" the trees he saw in June
1898 during his three-week visit to Japan. Having arrived in Yokohama, he
traveled to Tokyo by train along the old Tokaido road made famous by the
sketches of Utagawa Hiroshige (1797–1858), master of the Ukiyo-e school.
A seven-tiered plan used for the poem emphasizes the idea of heroic resist-
ance (the pine "resists"; it signifies "human resistance, with a struggle"),
though the poem will offer a more complex development; for it shows the
intimate correspondence of details of the landscape in the way of metaphors
of the same poem. As we read in *Art Poétique* "Everything that is, every-
where, designates that without which it could not have been."

The Golden Ark in the Forest

First publication: *Connaissance de l'Est*, 1900

Claudel had planned his short Japan trip well. Soon after arriving in Tokyo, he
left for Nikko, some thirty five miles away, to attend the annual religious feast
celebrated in the first days of June. The train goes via Utsonomiya, along the
road that the mikado's envoy took each year to pay solemn tribute to the shrine
of the shogun Tokugawa Ieyasu, buried there in 1617. "Yeddo" is the old name
for Tokyo; the houses are temples in the Nikko forest; the *torii* are the sacred
gates; Jingo, or rather Jimmu Tenno, the first sovereign of Japan, and the great-
great-grandson of the sun goddess Amaterasu Omikami, is the legendary earthly
ancestor of the imperial family; the *kagura* is the priest who performs Uzume's
sacred dance, and the name of the dance itself ("Joys of the Gods"), in front of
the cave of Amaterasu (evoked later in "The Deliverance of Amaterasu").

The Wanderer

First publication: *Connaissance de l'Est*, 1900

Claudel's walk in the forest between Nikko and Chuzenji in June 1898 was
invested by him with the prestige of an initiatory moment, to which he later

referred in his essay, "Connaissance du temps" of 1903. "Once, in Japan," he writes, "as I was climbing from Nikko to Chuzenji, I saw the green of a maple fulfill the harmony offered by a pine, the two trees being juxtaposed, though at a great distance, by the angle of my glance." He continues, "The present pages are a commentary on that forest text, the arborescent formulation, by way of June, of a new Poetic Art of the Universe, a new Logic." Bishamon, one of the seven Gods of Fortune, is traditionally represented in the armor of a samurai.

Here and There

First publication: *Mercure de France*, June 1899, under the title "Buddha"
The fourth, and last, of the Japanese texts of 1898 comprises six parts, as if the title referred to randomness. Nevertheless the words "here and there" may also be taken to typify for Claudel the mode and manner of Japanese art and thought, which his own poem formally espouses. Nihon Bashi is an area of Tokyo popular for its myriad shops, in particular those that retail traditional artware (it was once called "Curio Street" by foreigners). South of the capital, on the Pacific coast, is Shizuoka, where Claudel visited the Buddhist temple of Rinzaiji; still further south, in Kyoto, he saw the palace of the shoguns and mikados. The three thousand golden "Kwannon," or "Kannon," are images of the lord of mercy Avalokitesvara housed in a long temple; while the skull, or "wasted bubble," in the bosom of one huge statue is that of the mikado Go Shirokawa, who, in a former life, was a monk.

The Sedentary

First publication: *Mercure de France*, June 1899
His three weeks in Japan being at an end, Claudel returned to Shanghai. Before taking up a position as consul in Foochow, he spent three months in Shanghai, made difficult by professional problems. "The Sedentary" marks a time of taking stock. The "angelic science" mentioned in the last lines is the doctrine of Thomas Aquinas, the "Angelic Doctor"; while the "inexhaustible book" is Aquinas's *Summa Theologica*, of prime importance in Claudel's formulation of his *Art Poétique*.

The Land Viewed from the Sea

First publication *Connaissance de l'Est*, 1900

The poet sets out again; he is leaving Shanghai on his way to assume his new post. He sees himself as a perpetual traveler in body and spirit, "a man forever departing and never arriving."

Salutation

First publication: *Connaissance de l'Est*, 1900

Having returned to Foochow in September 1898, Claudel was exultant to take up once more his walks in a region he likened to the Biblical lands. "White Dogs" is the name of the islands at the mouth of the Min River, the lighthouse of which, on the night he arrived, shone like a greeting. He compares himself, as he walks in the land of grain and fruit, to Hylas seduced by the nymphs into whose waters he had dipped a pitcher.

The Suspended House

First publication: *Connaissance de l'Est*, 1900

Claudel first visited the monastery of Yong-fu in December 1896, where he wrote "The Contemplative." Now, nearly two years later, he goes back to spend a night in the frail wooden temple on the side of the cliff, but speaks as one who, year in and year out, observes a rule of contemplative existence.

The Spring

First publication: *Connaissance de l'Est*, 1900

A free moment in November 1898 allowed the poet to go sailing in a houseboat. Again he makes use of ancient Greek references: the grove of Parnassus, the Muses, the Castalian spring.

Noon Tide

First publication: *Connaissance de l'Est*, 1900

The swarming activity of Shanghai is caught in this page, which resonates with Claudel's love for the sea. "Camels" are here floats that increase the buoyancy of a heavily loaded vessel; "Madian" is a region bordering the Red Sea.

Peril of the Sea

First publication: *Connaissance de l'Est*, 1900

Claudel returned to Foochow from Shanghai in January 1899. The sea crossing lasted six days rather than two. On January 17 he wrote in his diary "I commend my soul to God." Eighteen years later, in January 1917, he set sail for Brazil on a diplomatic mission at a time when German submarines were having much success. He wrote "Ballade," one of his finest shorter poems in rhythmic and rhyming *versets*, in the course of the crossing. Again the journey becomes a spiritual one, but the temptation for the poet is now to throw himself into death-by-water like a total immersion or a dramatic self-immolation: "Rien que la mer éternelle pour toujours et tout à la fois d'un seul coup! La mer et nous sommes dedans! Il n'y a que la première gorgée qui coûte" ("Nothing but the eternal sea forever and suddenly in one instant! The sea and we are in it! Only the first mouthful is hard"). One can understand that Charles Péguy, a fellow Christian, might think of him as forever wanting to "cross abysses on a tight rope."

A Proposition on Light

First publication: *Mercure de France*, June 1899

Claudel had a predilection for this poem, which he sent to Paris for publication shortly after it was written. Stylistically unlike his previous Eastern texts, it shows the philosophical search for a unitary sense that undergirds his collection. He will later observe, "The world is not a chance heap of mixed entities but a living whole marked by solidarity in all its parts, an arrangement implying that each organ be harmoniously apportioned to achieve the orderly working of the whole."

Hours in the Garden

First publication: *Connaissance de l'Est*, 1900

Claudel tells of his gladness to go back to Foochow and his well-loved garden. The serial technique used in "Night on the Verandah," "Dreams," and "Hours in the Garden" allows him to compose a five-part prose elegy. Cadmus founded Thebes with five warriors who sprang from the dragon's teeth he had planted. The game of Goose is played with counters on a board divided into compartments, some of which bear the image of a goose.

Concerning the Brain

First publication: *Connaissance de l'Est*, 1900

Like the earlier pages on light, this text breaks with the apparent subject of *Knowing the East*, yet expresses a constant underlying preoccupation. Claudel later held these remarks to be so important that he reproduced them in his *Art poétique* and summarized the thought in the following terms: "I understand that, for man and other living beings, to live is to know. What is, then, the particular mode of one's knowledge of life? My vital, essential act is the elaboration of nervous vibration." In the last paragraph Claudel refers to the Aristotelian theory, developed by the Scholastics, according to which the soul is the body's subsistent form; and in a dialogue written forty years later ("Aegri Somnia"), he compares this concept to that of the Chinese vase: "All of Chinese philosophy and art turn on the vacuum. The vacuum in every human being is the mystical path . . . , everything is made of solidified light, this spiritual clay called porcelain. As fragile as a dream, as indestructible as an idea." To his poem he applies the Scholastic method: define, distinguish, deduce.

Leaving the Land

First publication: *Connaissance de l'Est*, 1900

After more than four years in China, Claudel left for France in October 1899. His poem encapsulates not merely his physical departure but a spiritual choice, which, he well knew, might entail his becoming a religious.

The Lamp and the Bell

First publication: *L'Occident*, November 1902

"God did not want me for a monastic life." Claudel returned to Foochow in early 1901. The first of his new poems, echoing his unsettled emotional life and pressing need to use time well, conjoins the polarities of lamp and bell.

The Deliverance of Amaterasu

First publication: *L'Occident*, November 1902

Two myths, one Chinese, the other Shinto, are woven together. The first is that of the Celestial Spinner and the Bullock Driver separated by the Milky Way: fate would seem to prevent the two constellatory lovers from meeting, but the Shuttle, or Moon, finds a way ("All things are thereby united in a secret intimacy"). The second is that of Amaterasu, goddess of the sun, who withdrew her light because she felt unloved but was tricked into returning by the eight hundred myriads of gods. The sacred *gohei* is a kind of wand or prayer stick decorated with paper streamers used for purification purposes at Shinto ceremonies; while Uzume's song is taken word for word from an article in English on the Shinto temple of Ise, Amaterasu's sanctuary.

Visit

First publication: *L'Occident*, November 1902

The poem commemorates a sedan-chair journey to visit the vice-roy, in the elite Black Mountain area of Foochow, to arrange for rice to be supplied during a drought. Claudel's mood is one of lonely exclusion. As Ysé says in *Partage de Midi* of 1905, "And I would ask him if he was happy, and he would look at me with his look of a failed priest."

Rice

First publication: *L'Occident*, November 1903

Claudel went to Indochina in February 1903 to seek regular trade between the French colony and Foochow, and his poem is a multivalent image of fructification.

The Full Stop

First publication: *L'Occident,* November 1903

The poet marks a time of self-appraisal like a full stop, a pause between the familiar and the strange, fire and darkness, life and death.

Libation to the Coming Day

First publication: *L'Occident,* November 1903

His visit to the region of Yong-fu, famous for its thermal springs, is the occasion for Claudel to develop the theme of sacrifice. Breaking with the gravity of "The Full Stop," he exults in a quasi-mystical buoyancy.

The Day of the Feast of All-Rivers

First publication: *L'Occident,* November 1903

The Foochow carnival of dragon boats took place on the fifth day of the fifth month of the Chinese calendar. The boats, each driven by a hundred paddlers, sported dragons' heads.

The Yellow Hour

First publication: *L'Occident,* May 1905

The last two poems, originally published together, form a manner of diptych. "The Yellow Hour" evokes a cereal splendor as blessed as the Biblical miracle of Cana, though an anxious note intrudes in the last line.

Dissolution

First publication: *L'Occident,* May 1905

Claudel returned to France in April 1905. This last poem, after the manner of the sacrament for the dead, is the most uniformly somber of the collection, for the loved woman "Ysé" has already sailed for Europe and thus "betrayed" their love. The East, so dear to him, and the sea he is crossing once more on his home voyage, dissolve into a lifeless mist.

The Lockert Library of Poetry in Translation

George Seferis: Collected Poems (1924–1995), translated, edited, and introduced by Edmund Keeley and Philip Sherrard

Collected Poems of Lucio Piccolo, translated and edited by Brian Swann and Ruth Feldman

C. P. Cavafy: Selected Poems, translated by Edmund Keeley and Philip Sherrard and edited by George Savidis

Benny Andersen: Collected Poems, translated by Alexander Taylor

Selected Poetry of Andrea Zanzotto, edited and translated by Ruth Feldman and Brian Swann

Poems of René Char, translated and annotated by Mary Ann Caws and Jonathan Griffin

Selected Poems of Tudor Arghezi, translated by Michael Impey and Brian Swann

"The Survivor" and Other Poems by Tadeusz Różewicz, translated and introduced by Magnus J. Krynski and Robert A. Maguire

"Harsh World" and Other Poems by Angel González, translated by Donald D. Walsh

Ritsos in Parentheses, translations and introduction by Edmund Keeley

Salamander: Selected Poems of Robert Marteau, translated by Anne Winters

Angelos Sikelianos: Selected Poems, translated and introduced by Edmund Keeley and Philip Sherrard

Dante's "Rime," translated by Patrick S. Diehl

Selected Later Poems of Marie Luise Kaschnitz, translated by Lisel Mueller

Osip Mandelstam's "Stone," translated and introduced by Robert Tracy

The Dawn Is Always New: Selected Poetry of Rocco Scotellaro, translated by Ruth Feldman and Brian Swann

Sounds, Feelings, Thoughts: Seventy Poems by Wisława Szymborska, translated and introduced by Magnus J. Krynski and Robert A. Maguire

The Man I Pretend to Be: The Colloquies" and Selected Poems of Guido Gozzano, translated and edited by Michael Palma, with an introductory essay by Eugenio Montale

D'Après Tout: Poems by Jean Follain, translated by Heather McHugh

Songs of Something Else: Selected Poems of Gunnar Ekelöf, translated by Leonard Nathan and James Larson

The Little Treasury of One Hundred People, One Poem Each, compiled by Fujiwara No Sadaie and translated by Tom Galt

The Ellipse: Selected Poems of Leonardo Sinisgalli, translated by W. S. Di Piero

The Difficulty Days by Roberto Sosa, translated by Jim Lindsey

US — 35A

Gate 40